What Would My Class Look Like If I Believed in Myself More?

What Would My Class Look Like If I Believed in Myself More?

Carolyn Orange

ROWMAN & LITTLEFIELD
Lanham • Boulder • New York • London

Published by Rowman & Littlefield
A wholly owned subsidiary of The Rowman & Littlefield Publishing Group, Inc.
4501 Forbes Boulevard, Suite 200, Lanham, Maryland 20706
www.rowman.com

Unit A, Whitacre Mews, 26-34 Stannary Street, London SE11 4AB

Copyright © 2016 by Carolyn Orange

All figures created by the author.

All rights reserved. No part of this book may be reproduced in any form or by any electronic or mechanical means, including information storage and retrieval systems, without written permission from the publisher, except by a reviewer who may quote passages in a review.

British Library Cataloguing in Publication Information Available

Library of Congress Cataloging-in-Publication Data

Names: Orange, Carolyn, author.
Title: What would my class look like if i believed in myself more? / Carolyn Orange.
Description: Lanham : Rowman & Littlefield, [2016] | Includes bibliographical references and index.
Identifiers: LCCN 2015047669 (print) | LCCN 2015051457 (ebook) | ISBN 9781475806519 (cloth : alk. paper) | ISBN 9781475806526 (pbk. : alk. paper) | ISBN 9781475806533 (electronic)
Subjects: LCSH: Teachers–Psychology. | Effective teaching. | Self-confidence.
Classification: LCC LB2840 .O73 2016 (print) | LCC LB2840 (ebook) | DDC 371.102–dc23 LC record available at http://lccn.loc.gov/2015047669

∞™ The paper used in this publication meets the minimum requirements of American National Standard for Information Sciences—Permanence of Paper for Printed Library Materials, ANSI/NISO Z39.48-1992.

Printed in the United States of America

Contents

Preface ix

Acknowledgments xvii

PHASE I: DISCONNECT: EXPLORING THE ROOTS OF SELF-DOUBT

1 Self-Doubt: Viewing You through a Deficit Lens 3

    Exercise 1.1: Silencing Negative Childhood Whispers 8
    Exercise 1.2: How Do You Compare? 9
    Exercise 1.3: Steps for Arresting Your Fears 10
    Exercise 1.4: Uprooting the Roots of Doubt 11

2 Self-Exploration: Assessing Strengths and Weaknesses as a Teacher 13

    Exercise 2.1: Strategies for Becoming a Wasabi Pea 22
    Exercise 2.2: Preparation Evaluation 23
    Exercise 2.3: Developing a Stress-Free Model of Teaching 24

3 Kicking the Habits That Nurture Doubt 25

    Exercise 3.1: Are You a Hostage to Self-Doubt? 34
    Exercise 3.2: Sweep Away Your Mind Clutter 35

PHASE II: RECONNECT: REPAIR AND RECONSTRUCT THE DAMAGE CAUSED BY NEGATIVE THOUGHTS

4   Getting a New Doubt-Averse Attitude: Replacing Fear with Trust   39

     Exercise 4.1: Reflections of Truth: Take a Closer Look   46
     Exercise 4.2: Check Your "Self-Efficacy"   47
     Exercise 4.3: Procrastination-Busting Strategies to Get You on a Roll   48

5   Jump-Starting Your Teacher Efficacy   49

     Exercise 5.1: Piecing Together Best Practices for Better Teaching   63
     Exercise 5.2: Part I for Evidence-Based Teaching Evaluations   65
     Exercise 5.2: Part II for Evidence-Based Teaching Evaluations   66
     Exercise 5.2: Part III for Evidence-Based Teaching Evaluations   67
     Exercise 5.3: Blueprint for Managing Risks Associated with Uncertainty   68

6   Managing the Brute Creations of Negative Emotions   69

     Exercise 6.1: Anger Response Analysis   80
     Exercise 6.2: Red Heat Rating   81
     Exercise 6.3: Lose the Baggage of Negative Thinking and Reclaim Your Positive Thinking   82

PHASE III: NEW CONNECTS: GENERATING NEW THINKING AND CONNECTING TO THE SUPER TEACHER WITHIN

7   Moving beyond Doubt to Enlightenment: Getting to Know the Professional You Better   85

     Exercise 7.1: Developing Interpersonal and Intrapersonal Skills   90
     Exercise 7.2: Assessing Your Star Teacher Persona   92

8   Creating Exceptional Educational Environments for Maximum Learning   93

     Exercise 8.1: Create a Tangential Learning Sequence Script   101
     Exercise 8.2: Create a Greenhouse Classroom   102

9   Exploring the Potency of Empowerment   103

     Exercise 9.1: Releasing the Sweet Fruits of Power in You and Your Students   111

Exercise 9.2: Unmasking Your Doubts and Your Students' Doubts
   with a Can-Do Attitude ... 112
Exercise 9.3: Blast Off Your Emotional Intelligence Skills in 5 Days ... 114
Exercise 9.4: How Do Your Leadership Skills Stack Up? ... 116

10 Changing Inside and Out: Necessary Steps for Being the Best ... 117

Exercise 10.1: Formulary for Change in Education ... 127
Exercise 10.2: Color Your Inner Charismatic Chameleon for Change ... 128
Exercise 10.3: Assessment of Teacher Tech Savvy in a Digital Age ... 129
Exercise 10.4: Change Your Future Possibilities with
   Positive Affirmations ... 130

Index ... 133

About the Author ... 141

Preface

Teachers are usually excited about their first opportunity to teach. As they think of becoming teachers, they dream rosy thoughts about their classrooms and wonder what it will be like when they one day have a classroom of their own. Unfortunately, for many of them, dark clouds of self-doubt dot the horizon and obscure the sunrise of their new teaching careers. What is self-doubt, and why is it important?

Self-doubt is a lack of faith, confidence, or belief in oneself that has many faces, such as being undecided, uncertain, skeptical, disbelieving, distrusting, questioning, or fearful. Self-doubt that is deeply rooted in fear can be immobilizing, undermine confidence, discourage positive thinking, and delay action. Self-doubt can be a shackle on the brain that restricts creative thought and inhibits risk taking by making one hesitate and waver rather than act. In a nutshell, self-doubt is a minimizer and can keep teachers from believing in themselves and from being the best teachers that they can be.

ORGANIZATION

This book is organized into 10 chapters by a three-step believe-in-yourself process. Step 1 is the *disconnect phase*, where the task is to identify sources of doubt and disconnect existing negative thoughts and messages in the first three chapters. Chapters 1 to 3 also address various aspects of expelling sources of doubt, such as examining the origins of doubt by reconstructing the shame and doubt of the past, ascertaining the underlying causes of doubt and impeding thoughts and discarding old beliefs, behaviors, messages, and thoughts as they relate to teaching.

Step 2 is the *repair and reconnect phase*, where frayed, troubling, or negative thoughts are repaired or refurbished through reexamination and revision of core beliefs, attitudes, and values and by managing negative emotions and developing interpersonal and intrapersonal skills. Chapters 4 to 6 address dismantling old thoughts and behaviors and refurbishing/reconnecting negative, troubling thoughts as they relate to teaching.

Step 3 is the *new connect phase*, where, similar to the way the brain grows new dendrites and connections, the person forms new connections via personal empowerment, new thoughts and attitudes, and a willingness to change, learn, and do new things. Chapters 7 to 10 focus on new thoughts, empowerment, and change as they relate to teaching.

RELEVANCE FOR APPROPRIATE AUDIENCES

Examples of other teachers' experiences with self-doubt are featured throughout this book. Tips on how to use the three-step believe-in-yourself process are included. This book is intended as a supplemental text that is a useful addition to any educator's professional library. It will be especially useful for preservice and beginning teachers who are looking for resources to help them become more proficient in their jobs.

Veteran teachers will find it useful in their efforts to improve their teaching and feelings of teacher efficacy. Administrators will have a resource that will guide them in the understanding and planning of personal and professional development for their teachers. They also will learn the importance of supporting teacher efforts to empower themselves, boost their confidence, and enhance their self-images. Most administrators will acquire a higher level of sensitivity to teacher doubts and will be better equipped to address them.

This book also is useful for any education-related course or workshop. College professors will find it a practical resource for examining preservice teachers' self-doubts and offering effective suggestions for overcoming them. The benefit is sending better-prepared teachers into the field. Professors also will be able to enhance their lectures to encourage their students to reflect on teacher doubt and strategies for enhancing self-confidence in teaching.

The topic of self-doubt is universal and is relevant for educators of all cultures. Therefore, the need for strategies to minimize doubt, empower teachers, and enhance teacher efficacy is needed by most educators, regardless of country of origin.

THE GOAL OF THIS BOOK

The goal of this book is to foster belief in oneself and move an educator from self-doubt to self-assurance in three phases that are inspired by the way a flawed brain is renewed. This idea is analogous to the notion of brain plasticity. The brain has an innate ability to renew itself, reshape itself, and increase in complexity with the proper learning experiences. The strategies presented in this book represent a three-step believe-in-yourself process that is analogous to the brain's capacity to undergo renovation.

Through self-examination, introspection, self-enrichment by augmenting knowledge, intellectual abilities, spiritual resources, and other skills, educators can reinvent themselves. Belief in oneself is directly proportional to one's ability to adapt by discarding old ideas, modifying existing ideas, and generating new ones.

INTRODUCTION: REAL-WORLD DOUBTS

Both new and veteran teachers experience self-doubt on occasion. For some, the experience is fleeting; for others, self-doubt establishes residency in the mind of its host and feeds heartily on negative perceptions, messages, and comments from negative people. Inevitably, self-doubt undermines self-assurance and productivity. Both new and veteran teachers tend to focus their self-doubts on their performance in the classroom, questioning their ability to handle disruptive students, manage difficult parents, and deal with unmotivated students.

Preservice Teaching Survey

The following survey results of 50 preservice teachers provide some evidence that the self-doubt process begins with the prospect of a job search, where preservice teachers are concerned about the likelihood of securing a teaching position. Getting a teaching job was the number one concern on the list of self-doubts expressed by the group. Being an effective teacher was number two on the list and reflects the type of self-doubt this book is addressing. All responses are listed below and ranked. Where there are multiple items tied for a rank, they are combined and listed under the same number:

First Place

- Finding a teaching job and getting hired.

Second Place

- Being an effective teacher. (Will I be able to teach them what they need to know and help them understand the materials?)

Third Place

- Being able to manage and control the classroom or getting a class that I can't handle that will make me want to quit.
- Afraid that I won't know the necessary material or content, such as grammar (being able to appropriately break down the content to the student's level or being able to analyze the educational material in depth).
- Concerned that I won't be able to be creative because I have to teach to the test. (I may become complacent if I have to teach to the test. Can I survive yearly testing? It's boring.)

Fourth Place

- Keeping feelings of stress and frustration under control. (Will I be an impatient teacher or short-tempered? Can I be flexible?)

Fifth Place

- Being able to keep students interested (being creative enough).
- Being able to handle inclusion of special needs children (differentiation).
- Will I have the stamina to handle the mental and physical drain of teaching (the workload and being able to last through the years).
- Will I be able to make learning fun? (Will students enjoy my class? Can I make the learning process more enjoyable and interactive?)

Sixth Place

- Will I be motivated enough to wake up so early in the morning, every morning?
- Concerned that I may not know how to react to a troubled student or respond to problem children.
- Ability to deal with discipline problems (disruptive class).
- Concern with passing the teacher certification test.
- Being able to engage my students in ways that will help them use what I teach them (keeping the students' attention).

Seventh Place

- Getting enough support from other teachers, administrators, and staff.
- Being able to adjust my thinking to that of the student.
- Ability to control my caring so that it is not too much.

- Performing adequately when being observed by the principal.
- Coping with students who don't want to learn (who have no interest in school or learning).
- Will I be prepared enough to teach?
- Will I be able to handle the age-group that I want to teach (i.e., older children)?
- I am afraid that I won't be respected because of my young age.
- I am afraid of my inability to handle school violence.
- I have a lack of experience with school policies and rules.
- Will I have the ability to teach a multicultural classroom?
- Will I be able to handle the responsibility of the children's learning?
- My confidence in being able to motivate my students.
- Will my lesson plans flow well?
- I am afraid that I might not like or believe what I teach.
- Do I have the ability to handle parent interference or parents' disengagement?
- Will I be able to effectively manage my time?
- Will I be able to negotiate a salary that is fair?
- Will I be able to be fair and unbiased?
- Will I measure up favorably when compared to other teachers?
- Will I be able to be friendly and not too stern?

The proliferation of self-doubts presented above illustrate that self-doubt has a broad brushstroke that covers many areas of the academic canvas. Helsing (2007) reports that there is a growing body of literature that examines the uncertain nature of teaching. Bandura (1997) proposes that insidious doubts can undermine even the most proficient of teachers. The preservice teachers in this survey seem to be responding to the multitude of teaching uncertainties that are inherent in the profession. Veteran teachers were not included in the survey.

Veteran Teachers' Poll

However, in a less formal inquiry of veteran teachers in about four graduate education classes, variations of the following summary of doubts emerged:

- Will I be able to promote parent involvement?
- If I want to improve my teaching, am I too old to learn new things?
- Is it okay to smile before Christmas? I don't know if and when I am being too nice.
- Am I getting my point across to students so they can retain it?
- I may be too emotional and hard on my students; my nerves are rattled easily. Could I be in the wrong profession?

- I feel less than most teachers, and I prefer to just work alone. What would I say to them anyway?
- I am uncomfortable working with special needs kids. I don't know if my training is adequate. What if there is an emergency or crisis? I'm not sure I would know what to do.
- I probably should not resent the principal when he or she tries to have a say about our teaching, but I can't seem to help it and show it in little ways. Will I ever be able to just listen?
- When so many of my students are not performing, am I at fault, or are they just poor performers? How much of the problem should I own?
- My students know so much more than I do about computers and technology. I hesitate to use our in-class computers, and the students just beg to use them.
- I have always had a hard time keeping my records up to date and organized. I live in fear of a spontaneous request for a student's file.
- I wonder if I am not a good teacher.

These doubts will be addressed throughout the book.

RESEARCH ON SELF-EFFICACY

Although most teachers are required to have a degree, not all of them were confident, excellent students. The seminal work of Bandura (1977) on self-efficacy validated the assumption that people often create and foster perceptions of their capabilities. Self-efficacy, as defined by Bandura (1997), is a person's beliefs about how well he or she can successfully complete a task. He proposes that one's beliefs about personal competency are dependent not on actual abilities but rather on what one believes one can do. Thus, the beliefs that people have about themselves can affect how they feel and how they behave.

If they were lower achieving, they may have had low self-efficacy, which could have affected their performance as a college student and will most likely affect their perceptions of their ability to perform and their beliefs about their capabilities as a teacher. Researchers have established that most students with higher self-efficacy tend to work harder and persevere in challenging, difficult situations and set and achieve higher goals (Bandura, 1977; Schunk, 1991). These findings underscore the critical need for educators to develop a strong, positive belief in their capabilities as well as having the requisite skills to teach.

THE BENEFITS OF THIS BOOK

Educators will explore sources of their self-doubt and strategies for eradicating it. They will learn the following: to abolish habits that foster doubt, to adopt new habits that discourage doubt, to develop a more positive attitude, to confidently employ best practices, to manage their emotions, to boost their emotional IQ, and to develop effective interpersonal and intrapersonal skills. Some of the benefits are that educators would do the following:

- Become more empowered and less doubtful.
- Learn to rethink, reassess, and rechannel negative energy.
- Overcome fear that leads to denial of shortcomings and mistakes.
- Be exposed to a variety of effective techniques and strategies for enhancing their interpersonal and intrapersonal skills.
- Be better prepared to tend to the psychological needs of their students.
- Develop a heightened sense of self-efficacy and teacher efficacy.
- Increase their emotional IQ and develop better coping strategies to enhance their ability to effectively manage their emotions.
- Learn to be more in tune with their feelings, enabling them to better assess and cope with discipline problems to effect positive outcomes.
- Acquire a positive outlook that is virtually free of doubt.
- Develop higher self-concept and self-esteem and become more self-loving.

This book responds to the needs of educators to develop positive perceptions of their capabilities and to overcome self-doubt and teaching uncertainties that may interfere with their success as a teacher. Although doubts about one's abilities can also foster more collaboration, help seeking, sensitivity to diversity, increased motivation, and other changes for the better, Wheatley (2002) proposes that positive responses to doubt must be encouraged and learned in many cases.

Traditional teacher education programs do not teach strategies for empowerment, for overcoming self-doubt, and for many other interpersonal and intrapersonal skills necessary for teacher success. More focus has been on meeting students' educational and emotional needs, and, consequently, teachers' feelings and psychological needs are less of a priority.

However, the benefits of having emotionally healthy, positive, productive teachers are many; students, parents, administrators, and fellow teachers all reap those benefits. Researchers have found links between teacher efficacy and student efficacy (Goddard, Hoy, & Woolfolk Hoy, 2000). The benefits manifest as teachers who are forward looking and willing to try new techniques and strategies, teachers who believe that if they can "conceive it and believe it, they can achieve it"—"it" being whatever they make up their minds to try to do.

Positive, emotionally healthy, confident teachers offer improved quality of instruction and classroom climate. This book examines the dynamics of self-doubt and its effects on teacher performance in educational settings and personal interactions with others, such as parents, students, and administrators. This book is intended to broaden the scope of the traditional view of classroom management to include some of the interpersonal and intrapersonal needs of the teacher.

Most of us are familiar with the airplane scenario where the flight attendant cautions passengers to put their own oxygen masks on before attempting to give assistance to someone close to them. This scenario is a perfect metaphor for teachers trying to motivate and inspire young people. The metaphor illustrates the need for teachers to put on their own mask of confidence, efficacy, and emotional stability before attempting to put such masks on the children in their classes. Teachers need strategies and techniques that will help them quell their self-doubts and believe in themselves and their capabilities. Teachers have the power to create highly effective classrooms that are very conducive to learning if they believe they can.

REFERENCES

Bandura, A. (1977). Self-efficacy: Toward a unifying theory of behavioral change. *Psychological Review, 84*(2), 191–215.

Bandura, A. (1997). *Self-efficacy: The exercise of control* (10th ed.). New York: Freeman.

Goddard, R. D., Hoy, W. K., & Woolfolk Hoy, A. (2000). Collective teacher efficacy: Its meaning, measure and effect on student achievement. *American Educational Research Journal, 37*, 479–507.

Helsing, D. (2007). Regarding uncertainty in teachers and teaching. *Teaching and Teacher Education, 23*(8), 1317–1333.

Schunk, D. (1991). Self-efficacy and academic motivation. *Educational Psychologist, 26*(3), 207–231.

Wheatley, K. F. (2002). The potential benefits of teacher efficacy doubts for educational reform. *Teaching and Education, 18*, 5–22.

Acknowledgments

Dear Tisha,

My darling daughter, your departure from this earth dimmed my life lights and hurled me into a vortex of grief and despair that without the gift of your wonderful son would have been difficult to escape. The memory of your beautiful spirit, your brilliance and grace, has served as an inspiration for me to finish this book so that I could dedicate it to you. I hope you approve.

Love you forever,
Mama

I would like to thank Rachel Livsey, a former acquisitions editor and friend, for helping to lift my spirits and for encouraging me to continue to write. I wish her well in her new endeavors. I would also like to thank Nancy Evans, Caitlin Crawford, and Sarah Jubar for helping to shape my vision of this book and making it a reality.

I like to refer to Emily Gaston, my former graduate assistant, as "Excellent Emily" because she expertly helped me with editing and made suggestions for my first book and for this book. It was my good fortune to find her again, for this book, now that she has graduated and become a successful counselor and educator. Thank you, Emily, your expertise has been invaluable.

Phase I

DISCONNECT: EXPLORING THE ROOTS OF SELF-DOUBT

1

Self-Doubt
Viewing You through a Deficit Lens

Maybe I am bigger than that skinny, little reflection.

*Our doubts are traitors and make us lose the good we oft might win, by fearing to attempt.*a

—William Shakespeare

ORIGINS OF DOUBT: SILENCING THE WHISPERS OF NEGATIVE CHILDHOOD MESSAGES

The seeds of doubt are often planted early in life, donning the guise of a joke, kidding, or a nickname. Some people doubt themselves with intense fervor and fear because of a message they received as a child. For example, a parent tells the child, "I really love to hear you sing solo," and then jokingly adds, "so low that I cannot hear you." The child may have been very excited, thinking it was a compliment, only to be devastated by the sarcastic comment at the end. Such a childhood whisper could easily silence a person and make him or her doubt his or her ability to sing or speak in front of others.

Surely, the parent did not intend to have that type of effect on the child, but the action planted seeds of doubt in the child regardless of intentions. Many children, however, have heard childhood whispers of perceived inadequacies and shortcomings and were unaware of the damaging effect those whispers had on them, on into adulthood. Children are more literal in their thinking and process information at face value. Therefore, jokes, innuendo, and witty remarks may have unintentional consequences because of immature interpretations. Unfortunately, many adults are unaware that children process information differently than adults, as explained by Piaget (2007) in his book *A Child's Conception of the World*, particularly adult metaphors and other rhetoric that requires a higher level of thinking to process the message.

Children may live up to the label conveyed by negative childhood whispers and adjust their behavior accordingly. This effect is compounded when used with absolutes such as "You always do ———," "You never do anything right," or "Must you always get in trouble?" Such negative whispers can become a self-fulfilling prophecy, similar to the effect obtained by Rosenthal and Jacobson's (1968) work "Pygmalion in the Classroom."

Sometimes the label is so ubiquitous that the child cannot process it all and has no idea of when or where it should apply. Children process it with their child brains and apply the label to themselves in totally inappropriate or inaccurate scenarios. For example, when adults use the label "You are too fast" to describe a child's behavior, when the child perhaps shows too much initiative or rushes to do something without asking permission first, the label "too fast" may have a negative connotation for the child. This is particularly true when the child has an accident or breaks or burns something as a result of being "too fast." Consequently, when a child hears the negative whisper "too fast," he or she may feel doubtful, ashamed, and less willing to show initiative.

Fortunately, some teachers and parents who are aware of the stages of child development understand that children have a need to show initiative and to be industrious, as proposed by Erikson (1993). Those adults also realize that being "too fast" is probably a good trait; in fact, it probably means that the children involved were assuming responsibility, being innovative, or showing initiative. If their development was accelerated, they might be demonstrating these wonderful characteristics early. Adults have the power to mentally rewrite their negative childhood whispers as positive self-talk that will break the silence caused by any negative whispers.

Negative childhood whispers may also come from teachers and other adults in a child's life. For example, if a teacher made a comment such as "You talk so much that your lips are probably tired," the child may interpret that literally to mean that it is not good to talk and may be reluctant to participate in class rather than limiting his or her talking to a length of time that is more socially acceptable.

Teachers need to be aware of the potency of their casual remarks and to temper their responses, to be constructive and positive, and to make comments that empower rather than disparage. Adults affected by negative childhood whispers can undo some of the damage by sifting through their long-term memories to discover any childhood whispers that they may have encountered in their past. Being aware of the whispers and making a connection to current behavior and rejecting negative messages will be critical to silencing the whispers of those messages.

DO NOT COMPARE YOUR INSIDES TO THEIR OUTSIDES— YOU NEVER KNOW WHERE THEIR NEW SHOE PINCHES

Preservice teachers expressed a concern that they might not measure up when compared to other teachers. This rather latent fear may be due to "positioning," a mental exercise that many people participate in when they meet other people; they feel they must know where they stand in relation to others on many terms, such as wealth, social status, education, housing, occupation, and so on. After comparing notes gathered from bits and pieces of conversation, people often relegate themselves to a relative position of "better than," "about the same," or "less than."

Positioning may prove useful on a general level to avoid falling behind societal expectations of progress when compared to others, but specifically it is pointless because it is only a generalization and not necessarily the truth. For example, a woman wearing plain, inexpensive shoes that look nice might compare herself unfavorably to a woman wearing beautiful, more expensive shoes.

Outwardly, the new, beautiful shoes seem much better than the plain shoes, but actually the new, beautiful shoes have a serious flaw that makes the woman's feet hurt after wearing them. The truth is that the plain shoes are more valuable because they are very comfortable and compare very favorably to the painful, beautiful shoes, thereby eliminating the need for the plain-shoe owner to feel less than.

New teachers should avoid positioning and feel reasonably confident that they will measure up with the knowledge that other teachers may appear more competent and yet may have serious teaching flaws that are not evident. New teachers should have high expectations of success and believe they will be resourceful enough to manage any situation that might interfere with that success.

An inability to communicate with other teachers is another concern expressed by preservice teachers. Actually, their concern is more a matter of choice than a real concern. New teachers must elect to communicate to improve their probability of success when dealing with the myriad problems inherent in multidimensional classrooms. They can reduce their learning curve by learning from the experience of others. An intimidating aspect of communicating in education is the prolific number of programs strategies, acronyms, practices, and pedagogy that are part of everyday teacher speak. Buzzwords abound and may present the daunting task of trying to make sense of it all.

There are books and websites that can provide instruction. A quick reference guide for educational innovations (Orange, 2002) features explanations of buzzwords concerning practices, policies, programs, and so on that are widely discussed in education.

TACKLING AND PINNING DOWN DEBILITATING FEARS

Fear is a mental construct or a state of mind. Fear also is a choice; it does not have to manifest unless real physical or psychological danger is imminent. Sometimes we anticipate danger that may or may not become real, but nonetheless we experience all the symptoms of fear. Although the physiology of fear symptoms makes it feel real and palpable as the heart beats faster, palms feel sweaty, and nerve endings spark, it is important to acknowledge that such evidence only appears to be real fear. People can choose not to fear unless they see real danger and dismiss thoughts of fear if no real danger is present.

Fear can dissipate in a matter of seconds if the fear-provoking thought is replaced with a more pleasant or desirable thought. Dismissing fear thoughts does not mean ignoring a potentially dangerous situation; it simply means delaying a fear response until the danger is immediate. When nagging fears present themselves, replace them with dots of courage and contentment. Fear should not be so powerful that it overcomes or immobilizes a person. Channeling fear into hypervigilance, resourcefulness, and action is the way nature intended for people to respond when danger is present. Acceptance is the key for dispelling fears of bad outcomes that cannot be controlled.

All fears are not created equal. There are worries about the future or unpleasant outcomes that are fairly common. There are also uncommon features that can be debilitating. Both are a concern for teachers and preservice teachers. These fears can interfere with the person's efforts to effectively perform his or her work duties. Exploring fears is a useful first step for eradicating them.

EXPLORING THE ROOTS OF SELF-DOUBT AND UPROOTING THEM

The seeds of doubt planted in early childhood thrive in an environment that fails to foster self-esteem and boost the child's confidence. If children fail to develop a belief system that nurtures their perception of capability and resourcefulness, they may languish under a cloud of uncertainty into adulthood. Adults who wish to uproot their doubts must first explore their doubt feelings, ferreting out the root causes. Next, they should plan to eradicate those roots completely, much like a gardener would seek to eradicate the noxious roots of weeds in their gardens by destroying them completely so they cannot grow again.

For gardeners, extermination is simple: use a good weed killer that destroys roots, and the pesky weed problem is solved. For humans, uprooting a firmly entrenched root system that fuels doubt that has developed for years is more complicated. The roots of human doubt are buried in a simulated soil of a lack of knowledge and conviction, uncertainty, hesitation, misperceptions, fears, and so on. The roots of doubt are cognitive perceptions that fall into the following categories: people, events, situations, time, and self (PESTS). Eradicate doubt at the first sign, much like removing the weeds of the mind.

REFERENCES

Erikson, E. H. (1993). *Childhood and society.* New York: Norton.
Orange, C. (2002). *The quick reference guide to educational innovations: Practices, programs, policies, and philosophies.* Thousand Oaks, CA: Corwin.
Rosenthal, R., & Jacobson, L. (1968). Pygmalion in the classroom. *The Urban Review, 3*(1), 16–20.

Exercise 1.1: Silencing Negative Childhood Whispers

Instructions: This exercise involves taking a visual image trip through your childhood home(s) in a protective thought bubble. Nothing can penetrate the bubble and hurt you. Try to recall any negative childhood whispers, no matter how small or unimportant they may appear. Before you begin your trip, lie down in a comfortable, quiet place and relax. Make a mental note of all of the messages you can remember from the visual trip until you can no longer think of any other messages. Use the following diagram to help you map and process the messages that you have found. Rewrite the last column as positive messages or self-affirmations.

Silencing Negative Childhood Whispers with Self-Talk		
Person sending the message	**The Negative Whisper**	**Positive Self-Affirmations**
Father	"I love it when you sing solo... so low that I can't hear you. Ha Ha"	"I have a beautiful voice, many people love to hear me sing!"
Aunt		
Cousin		

 **Exercise 1.2: How do you compare?**

Instructions: Do you compare yourself to others? If so, list the names of the persons you compare yourself to and check the appropriate box to the right that indicates how you see yourself compared to each of those persons. The first item is marked as an example. Use additional paper if needed. Count the number of marked boxes in each category to get an overall measure of how you see yourself. How do you compare?

_____

If you mark more than one as "less than", List some ways that you compare favorably to the people you have listed and some actions you can take to improve yourself in the areas where you see yourself as less than._____

_____

Compared to __Gina__ I am	Less Than ■	About the Same ☐	Better Than ☐
Compared to _____ I am	Less Than ☐	About the Same ☐	Better Than ☐
Compared to _____ I am	Less Than ☐	About the Same ☐	Better Than ☐
Compared to _____ I am	Less Than ☐	About the Same ☐	Better Than ☐

 **Exercise 1.3: Steps for Arresting Your Fears**

Instructions: This exercise is useful for quieting fears and attaining serenity.

1. Identify any fears that you can recall feeling in the past few years and any that you are feeling now. Mentally summon a **peace officer** (Name someone you trust with your fears_____) and make a report when fears are disturbing your peace. Let the peace officer help you to arrest your fears.
2. Pick your fears out of a mental fears **line-up** and identify your most debilitating fears. Write them on the fear graphic below.

3. **Convict** your fears on the evidence of not being real. Write your evidence of not being real on the line provided. _____
   Look for evidence of your fears not being a real threat (for example, moonlight casting eerie shadows on the wall when shining on furniture. It is fear-inducing, but not real.
   _____
4. Confront your fears in a **court** of contentment.
   Make contentment statements such as: "It does not matter what other people think",
   _____, _____, _____.
   Choose positive replacement thoughts: "I can do this", _____,
   _____, _____.
5. Put your fears under **house arrest** with mental and physical peace aids:
   Mental aids such as visual imagery—imagine yourself doing the thing you fear or _____; and
   Physical aids such as—meditation, humming or chanting, and using worry beads or stones _____

Exercise 1.4: Uprooting the Roots of Doubt

Instructions: In the following exercise, identify and list some root causes, P.E.S.T.S. (people, events, situations, time, self) of doubt that pertain to you and give an example of each. Cross out the messages that you are willing to uproot and let go.

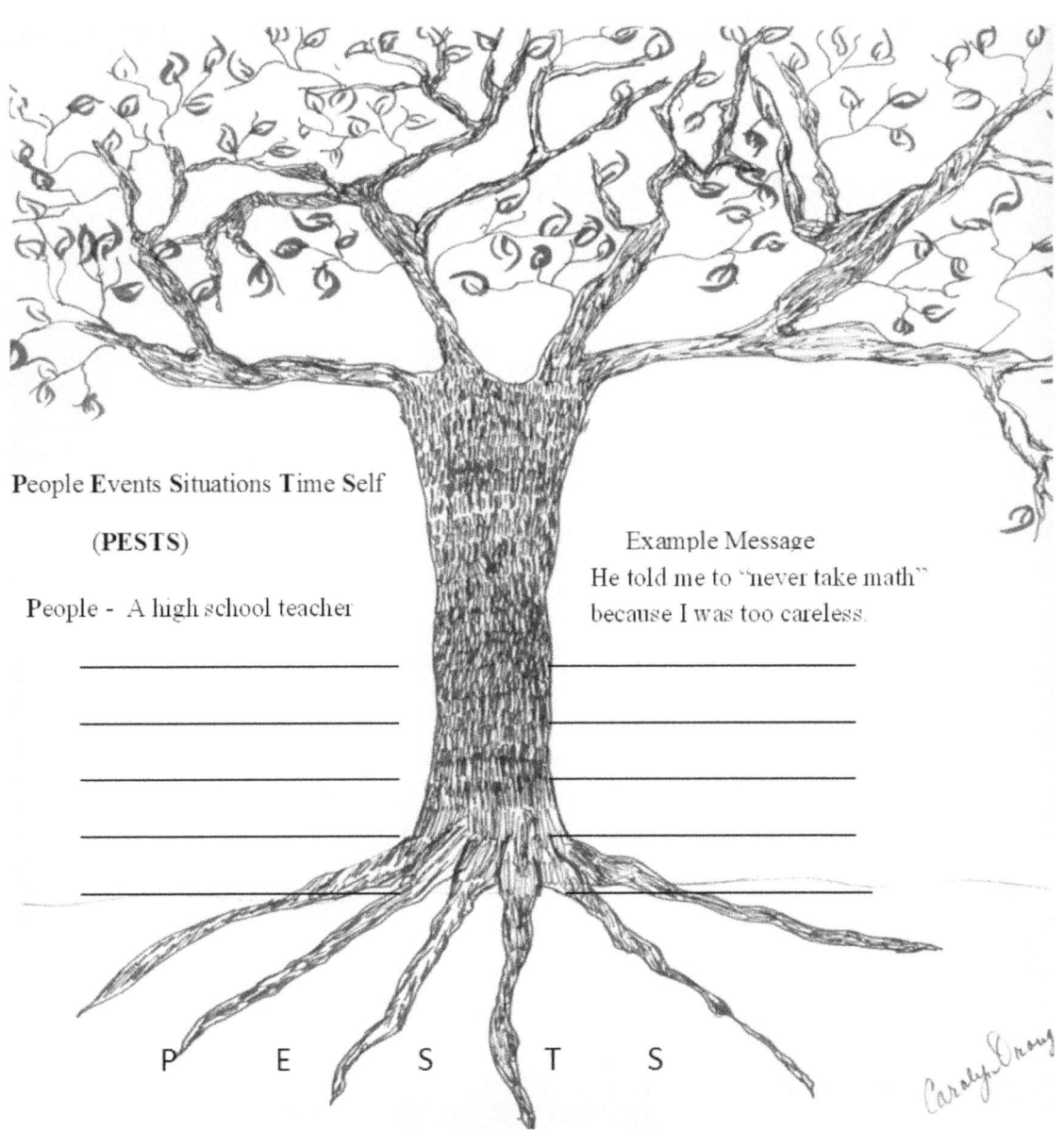

People Events Situations Time Self

(PESTS)

People - A high school teacher

Example Message
He told me to "never take math" because I was too careless.

P   E   S   T   S

2

Self-Exploration

Assessing Strengths and Weaknesses as a Teacher

After deep reflection, I've decided that being spotlessly neat can be an asset in the classroom.

The greatest weakness of all is the great fear of appearing weak.

—Jacques BeNigne Boussuet

IN PURSUIT OF GREAT TEACHER TRAITS

For years, there has been a quest to find the holy grail of teaching—the traits that distinguish great teachers from average teachers. Great teacher traits are comprised of talents, qualities, attributes, or behaviors that determine the high, average, or low caliber of teachers. Some of the traits are genetic, and some are acquired with hard work and concerted effort. Great teacher traits are derived from a variety of areas of human development: psychosocial, character, personality, cognitive, behavior, and physical. Great teachers who possess the following distinguishing traits are usually regarded as power teachers who deliver powerful teaching and create powerful learners.

Behavioral—Great teachers model the behavior they would like to see in their students. They model hard work and a commitment to lifelong learning. They possess high self-motivation and the ability to motivate or move their students to action. These teachers strive to make a difference and to have a powerful impact on their students' lives.

Character—It is not surprising that great teachers have very high quality character traits, such as honesty, with students, parents, and colleagues. Their power lies in their humility, which is often the backdrop of their character. They have reconciled the discrepancy between their actual and ideal selves to discover their true selves (Hamman et al., 2013).

Great teachers with character inspire confidence in their students (Bafirman, 2014). They are usually trustworthy and protective of tender student psyches; students feel psychologically safe with them. They don't have trust issues from their past, thereby eliminating a need for excessive control (Vajda, 2011). They know who they are in their educational spheres; discontent, dissatisfaction, and displaced anger are not options. They handle anger and other negatives appropriately with grace and understanding.

Cognitive—Great teachers, like other great thinkers, are intelligent, highly creative critical thinkers. The divergence of their thinking allows them to conceive a variety of solutions to a problem—solutions that are innovative and fresh. Such thinkers often possess sharpened skills of perception, giving them the ability to hear what is not being said or to read between the lines of conversations and respond appropriately.

Personality—High charisma and tolerance are certainly characteristics of great teachers. They are loving, caring, and respectfully embracing of their students' differences. Great teachers love learning and "infect" their students with the same love. They also love their students; they give praise and approval freely. Most of these teachers have a healthy, authoritative style of relating to students (Baker, Clark, Crowl, & Carlson, 2009). They are fair and ethical, treating all students equitably.

Great teachers possess a composite caring trait that makes them genuinely affectionate, sensitive, and empathic, feeling students' joys, pains, and apprehensions as they celebrate and commiserate with their students. Tolerance of students' shortcomings, peppered by their powers to empower students, is also a trait of great teachers.

Psychosocial—Great teachers are affable and aspire to a life that is free of mental and spiritual defects of the mind, body, and spirit. They strive to avoid substance abuse, alcoholism, or overeating; they opt for a healthy lifestyle. They seek help for medical conditions that can interfere with their teaching effectiveness. Mental illness is a hindrance and a potential hazard to others unless controlled by medication and proper treatment; great teachers are committed to optimal mental health and adhere to their treatment regimens or resign if they feel they cannot manage their medical condition or mental illness. They are usually emotionally stable and reasonably happy, taking their mistakes and the mistakes of others in stride.

Professional—Consummate professionalism is a power mantra for great teachers. These teachers know what students need and are willing to nurture them and meet their needs and goals. They are able to go beyond the classroom to build community with their students. Within this community, they have high expectations for all students; they intuitively know what resources and tools are needed to achieve their learning objectives or outcomes.

They are resourceful and can visualize items that will be useful for explaining concepts. They also can see items or artifacts outside the classroom and immediately make a brain connection for their use in the classroom to make their teaching more alive and vibrant.

Great teachers put forth superior effort in their classroom preparation, often coming in early and sometimes staying late. They use their planning period for planning, not personal free time.

Great teachers are extraordinarily competent and derive immense pleasure from watching learning take place. They appreciate order and like having a place for everything and having everything in its place. They are able to execute all aspects of excellent teaching by keeping themselves aware of the best teaching practices and by viewing teaching as meaningful, satisfying work, not only a job.

ASSESSING PROFESSIONAL SKILLS AND QUALITY OF TEACHER PREPARATION

A source of teacher doubt is the dissonance that manifests between what teachers were taught in teacher education classes and the complexities of actual classroom teaching. Many novice teachers are intimidated by their lack of preparation in important areas of teaching. The multidimensionality of classroom teaching demands that teachers be well prepared to be effective. The following list offers teachers strategies and tips for addressing aspects of the various dimensions of teaching:

Interrelating with Administration and Colleagues

- Collegiality—Be willing to share ideas and resources with coworkers.
- Mentoring—Be teachable; learn from master teachers and mentors.
- Meetings—Acquire knowledge of meeting protocols, such as Robert's Rules of Order.
- Professional development—Develop metacognitive strategies for remediating areas of weakness in teaching.
- Technical development—Become more tech savvy; learn new ways to include digital learning and stay current through continuing education.
- Duties—Acquire knowledge of various types of noninstructional tasks that teachers are required to perform.

Observing School Rules and Policies

- Levels of school rules—Acquire knowledge of rules at the district, school, and classroom levels to avoid inadvertently violating a rule (Woolfolk, 2013).
- Unwritten rules—Make sure your behaviors and comments in a school setting are politically correct.
- Policy on bullying—Be aware of and in compliance with the school district's tolerance level and response to bullying behavior.
- Sexual harassment—Understand and abide by what the district considers inappropriate behaviors between coworkers, students, or administrators (Orange, 2008).

Interacting with Parents

- Parent involvement—Acquire knowledge of strategies for including parents in their child's education; plan to showcase students' talents and work to attract parents to the classroom.
- Communication with parents—Be aware of the many ways of contacting parents, such as electronically, in writing, in person, or by phone.
- Parent conferences—Knowledge of successful strategies for conducting parent conferences, such as getting student deficiencies to the parent sandwiched between layers of praise.
- Parent conflicts—Acquire knowledge of how to diffuse parent anger, identify the problem, and work with the parent to resolve the problem.
- Parent visits—Acquire knowledge of how to handle unexpected visits from parents if they are not screened by the main office before coming to your classroom.

Cultivating the Classroom Environment

- Climate or culture—Develop a climate of mutual respect, understanding, and courtesy (Patrick, Kaplan, & Ryan, 2011).
- Organization—Use the most functional room layouts and arrangement of contents to meet the needs of the students.
- Decor or appearance—Develop a flair for interesting, attractive learning-based room decorations.
- Functionality—Learn how to set up a well-designed classroom to best handle movement, transitions, and consistent monitoring of activities.
- Supplies and resources—Maintain adequate inventories of needed supplies and know where to seek a source of needed resources.

Operative Lesson Planning

- Behavioral or learning objectives (Gronlund, 1991)—Learn to specify the why, or the purpose, of every assignment and the expected learning outcomes to avoid assigning busywork.
- Creating and administering tests—Make sure that teacher-made tests are relevant, reliable, and fair.
- Grading or assessment—Use rubrics for more objective grading.
- Homework or seat work—Determine the need inappropriateness of homework assignments and seat work.

Effective Lesson Delivery

- Presentation—Use correct grammar, effective visuals, adequate voice control, and body language to create effective presentations.
- Communication—Clearly communicate instructions and what is expected of students.
- Timing and pacing—Pause often when presenting lesson material to allow students time to absorb the material.
- Questioning—Create effective questions that encourage critical thinking rather than a rote response of yes or no.

Competent Student Management

- Discipline—Develop appropriate strategies for handling disrespect and disruption professionally and appropriately.

- Reward or incentives—Acquire knowledge of developmentally appropriate rewards and reward schedules.
- Student engagement (Woolfolk, 2013)—Monitor and maximize the use of allocated time for interesting and relevant assignments.
- Motivation—Create exciting, challenging activities that are relevant to student interests and move them to action.
- Skills assessment—Plan assessment that addresses strengths and weaknesses through differentiation or individualized instruction (Tomlinson, 1999).
- Rapport—Establish and maintain a courteous, caring, supportive relationship with students.

Proficient in Student Personnel Matters

- Student attendance records—Keep well-organized, timely, and updated records.
- Standardized tests—Know and abide by testing protocols to avoid introducing bias and be able to accurately explain test results to parents.
- Individualized education plan (Orange, 2002)—Acquire knowledge of how to guide the delivery of special services for special needs students.
- Special needs—Acquire knowledge of how to arrange the classroom and activities to accommodate students with disabilities or challenges.

AVOIDING STRESS AND ANXIETY

Stress overload can easily translate into a distressed body state that is more susceptible to myriad health disorders. Establishing a healthy line of defense is imperative for teachers to avoid the negative consequences of stress. A physically fit, emotionally stable, instruction-savvy professional is well equipped to weather the stress storm of teaching under the worst teaching conditions. Unfortunately, most teachers fail to meet all of these conditions and are therefore vulnerable to the ravages of stress. Some stress in teaching is inevitable. A strategy involving prevention, awareness, and remediation will be useful for bringing teachers up to par for building a healthy line of defense.

Prevention necessitates eating right, avoiding stimulants, exercising, and getting quality sleep. Eating right is best accomplished by avoiding high-sugar and high-fat foods, particularly in large quantities. Alcohol, caffeine, drugs, and even prescription drugs can have an effect on a teacher's cognitive abilities and should be avoided or used only as prescribed. Exercise increases strength endurance and releases feel-good chemicals, such as serotonin and endorphins, that can minimize stress. Adequate, restful sleep without the assistance of sleep aids is necessary to avoid the brain fog and accompanying sleep deprivation that can interfere with a teacher's ability to deliver quality instruction.

Awareness is being vigilant about internal and external conditions that are not conducive to one's well-being. Stressors associated with instruction, classroom management, school policies, and societal pressures are a good place to start using strategies to alleviate stress. When teachers start to feel overloaded with work, responsibilities, or expectations, they should immediately seek ways to pare down their workload to diminish its negative effects. All teachers should be comfortable with help seeking and with saying no to unreasonable requests; they also should be open to new ideas and proven, successful approaches to problems.

All teachers should learn to recognize personal signals of stress, such as anxiety (Johns, 1992); insomnia; obsessing at night; depression; problems with the heart, breathing, or blood pressure; irritability; reactivity; and impulsiveness. They should consider the causes of their symptoms and seek calming, remedial techniques to ease them.

Remediation can be accomplished in most of the stress areas associated with teaching. Remedy stress associated with instruction by teaching engaging lessons, by minimizing volunteering time (i.e., before and after school), and by doing long-range planning to avoid uncertainty. Developing an understanding of children's developmentally appropriate behavior, a repertoire of instructional strategies, and discipline strategies will minimize stressors associated with these potential sources of stress.

The stress of teacher evaluations can be minimized by soliciting the feedback of administrators and students before time for evaluations and thereby correcting areas of weakness before an actual evaluation. Avoiding self-defeating beliefs and behaviors and focusing on delivering the best possible instruction for every class taught should alleviate much evaluation apprehension. To prepare for stressful situations, develop and test a repertoire of strategies and techniques that are research based to be prepared for whatever pedagogical problems might arise.

If teachers collaboratively set up rules with their students and agree on reasonable consequences, students will be more likely to comply; additionally, being fair, kind, and consistent about compliance to the rules in the context of interesting, engaging, enlightening lessons will minimize potential stress. Effectively avoiding an environment that is conducive to negative teacher–pupil interactions is ideal because there will be less unacceptable student behavior and less frustration and teacher anger, which often result in aberrant teacher behavior.

A lack of administrative support can be stress inducing. To increase administrative support, teachers should schedule a face-to-face meeting to discuss their needs and expectations and get an assessment of how administrators feel they can best accommodate teachers' needs. Administrators also should offer alternative solutions for needs that they feel they cannot meet. Such a meeting brings down the curtain of uncertainty and avoids stress.

Increased professional development may be the solution for alleviating the stress of teacher accountability. The more skills teachers have, the better able they are to successfully handle the variety of demands placed on them in teaching, and the likelihood that they will successfully meet those demands increases. Teachers who identify and structure their core beliefs to accommodate positive perceptions and attitudes will create less stressful learning environments that are nurturing for themselves and their students.

Teachers who finance student supplies and activities out of their own pockets may experience the creeping stress of whether this will ever end and how much this will cost. Businesses are starting to recognize that teachers have ever-mounting out-of-pocket educational expenses, and some are offering programs to reduce teacher expenditures. Teachers can minimize their financial stress by seeking assistance from these types of programs. To avoid stress, teachers also should use self-empowerment techniques and tell themselves that they don't have to be extraordinary to be good teachers.

There is much to be gained from minimizing stress for teachers and for students. Teachers should manage their stress levels and model them after tides on a beach; let them be like gentle waves that rise, fall, quickly retreat, and dissipate to calm waters.

REFERENCES

Bafirman. (2014). Influence of sports, physical education and health teacher professionalism in developing students' character. *Asian Social Science, 10*(5), 7.

Baker, J. A., Clark, T. P., Crowl, A., & Carlson, J. S. (2009). The influence of authoritative teaching on children's school adjustment: Are children with behavioural problems differentially affected? *School Psychology International, 30*(4), 374–382.

Gronlund, N. E. (1991). *How to write and use instructional objectives* (Vol. 4). New York: Macmillan.

Hamman, D., Coward, F., Johnson, L., Lambert, M., Zhou, L., & Indiatsi, J. (2013). Teacher possible selves: How thinking about the future contributes to the formation of professional identity. *Self and Identity, 12*(3), 307.

Johns, K. M. (1992). Lowering beginning teacher anxiety about parent-teacher conferences through role-playing. *The School Counselor, 40*(2), 146–152.

Orange, C. (2002). *The quick reference guide to educational innovations: Practices, programs, policies, and philosophies*. Thousand Oaks, CA: Corwin.

Orange, C. (2008). *25 biggest mistakes teachers make and how to avoid them*. Thousand Oaks, CA: Corwin.

Patrick, H., Kaplan, A., & Ryan, A. M. (2011). Positive classroom motivational environments: Convergence between mastery goal structure and classroom social climate. *Journal of Educational Psychology, 103*(2), 367–382.

Tomlinson, C. A. (1999). *The differentiated classroom: Responding to the needs of all learners*. Alexandria, VA: Association for Supervision and Curriculum Development.

Vajda, P. (2011). The voices of fear, doubt and mistrust. http://www.management-issues.com/opinion/6302/the-voices-of-fear-doubt-and-mistrust

Woolfolk, A. E. (2013). *Educational psychology* (12th ed.). Boston: Pearson Education.

Exercise 2.1: Strategies for Becoming a **Wasabi Pea**

Instructions: The following P-characteristics are important for effective teaching. Think of them as a personal can of success peas. When a Wasabi condiment is added to peas, the result is a strong, pungent experience, way beyond the scope of the ordinary sweet pea. Great teachers want to be strong, stimulating and powerful. They want to be a Wasabi Pea! Write some strategies that you can employ as a teacher to make your P-characteristics very powerful, potent, and beneficial to your students. Some examples are provided for you; add to them and fill in the ones that are blank.

Prepared-Plan to be effective; have everything needed for instruction organized and ready to go.
Professional
Patience
Persevering
Praising-Give honest praise freely and celebrate every moment of student success with gusto.
Passionate-Love your work, love your students and love yourself.
Pleasant
Polite-Model the good manners you would like to see in your student at all times!
Playful-Laugh and play with students at every appropriate opportunity; enjoy them.
Positive
Personable-Be approachable; plan one-on-one opportunities for all of your students, often.
Practical
Powerful-Be a daily dreamer, visualize your students as successful in spite of life circumstances.
Proactive
Punctual
Peaceful-Create a safe, nurturing environment for all students and yourself; say no to frustration.
Performing
Perceptive-See teaching for what it is, deep, meaningful work that demands full attention.
Particular
Pliant
Poised
Productive-Accomplish much as you try many new things and complete them successfully.

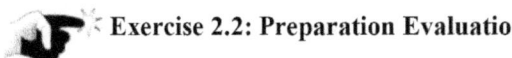 **Exercise 2.2: Preparation Evaluation**

Instructions: Using the list of skills below, give yourself 10 points, by putting a "+" sign on the line in front of the number 10, for every skill you learned as a part of your teacher education program. Deduct 10 points by putting a "-" sign on the line in front of the number 10, for the skills you were not taught or that were not addressed in your teacher education courses. Tally up the subtotals of +10s and -10s to reveal your score. Refer to the explanation of scores below to determine if you are underprepared, adequately prepared, or expertly prepared.

Administration & Colleagues		School Rules and Policies		Classroom Environment		Parents	
__10	Collegiality	__10	Levels of rules	__10	Climate	__10	Involvement
__10	Mentoring	__10	Unwritten rules	__10	Organization	__10	Conferences
__10	Meetings	__10	Bullying	__10	Decor	__10	Conflict
__10	Duties	__10	Sexual	__10	Functionality	__10	Communication
__10	Professional Development	__10	harassment Substitutes	__10	Supplies & Resources	__10	Parent Development
Subtotals +__ -__		Subtotals +__ -__		Subtotals +__ -__		Subtotals +__ -__	
Lesson Planning		Lesson Delivery		Student Personnel Matters		Classroom Management	
__10	Teacher tests	__10	Presentation	__10	Attendance	__10	Discipline
__10	Rubrics	__10	Communication	__10	Student IEP	__10	Rapport
__10	Homework	__10	Timing/Pacing	__10	Grading	__10	Motivation
__10	Lesson Plan	__10	Questioning	__10	Special Needs	__10	Rewards
__10	Learning objectives	__10	Differentiation	__10	Standardized Testing	__10	Skills Assessment
Subtotals +__ -__		Subtotals +__ -__		Subtotals +__ -__		Subtotals +__ -__	

Total Score _____

400 to 300 = Expertly Prepared   290 to 190 = Adequately Prepared   ≤ 180 = Underprepared

Explanation of scores: If you are underprepared, some teacher refresher courses or additional educational courses may be needed.

If you are only adequately prepared and you wish to be a great teacher, professional development activities will make you a better than adequate teacher.

If you are expertly prepared, congratulations . . . for now. Remember education is in a constant state of reform. To maintain your expert status, stay abreast of current developments.

Exercise 2.3: Developing a Stress-free Model of Teaching

Instructions: Teachers would benefit from adopting a more nurturing teaching model that would help them to avoid frustration and anger. Write examples of ways you can employ the following suggestions in your teaching experiences.

Focus on helping students, rather than internalizing personal feelings about their misbehavior.

Your Examples:

Be reasonably accessible to students and administrators; guard your personal time.

Your Examples:

Avoid tasks having super human expectancies; just say no.

Your Examples:

Allow yourself to make mistakes and learn from them.

Your Examples:

Make sure every student gets an opportunity to experience some success.

Your Examples:

Nurturing students and using kind words is a way to maintain discipline.

Your Examples:

Try to understand student misbehavior before acting.

Your Examples:

Create a learning environment where everyone can safely take risks.

Your Examples:

Be willing to give students a second chance and an opportunity to rethink their misbehavior.

Your Examples:

3

Kicking the Habits That Nurture Doubt

See, we've crossed the street. Next time don't listen when others tell you that snakes need legs to cross the street.

> *One of the reasons it has seemed so difficult for a person to change his habits, his personality, or his way of life, has been that heretofore nearly all efforts at change have been directed to the circumference of the self, so to speak, rather than to the center.*
>
> —Maxwell Maltz

RECOGNIZING HABITS THAT MAKE YOU A HOSTAGE TO DOUBT

One of the intricacies of the complex human brain is that it can easily be held hostage by habits that foster self-doubt. Habits are stealthy in that they arise from an unconscious pattern of behavior that is strengthened by repetition. People become hostages to self-doubt because when faced with certain situations, their default, habitual reaction is to doubt themselves. Self-doubt is the antithesis of self-efficacy, or a person's belief in their abilities or capacities (Bandura, 1977).

For educators, this same belief as it pertains to education is referred to as teacher efficacy (Woolfolk Hoy, Rosoff, & Hoy, 1990). Paulus and Scherff (2008) conducted a study of 15 preservice teachers. They analyzed their participants' online dialogue and inductively determined that participants' stories were about self-doubt or self-efficacy, more specifically, teaching efficacy, with a focus on teaching inadequacy. Recognizing and eliminating habits that set teachers up for self-doubt is important for building self-efficacy and teacher efficacy.

There are seven common habits that can tether the brain to self-doubt:

1. Listening to incompetent others or asking for advice before making a move
2. Seeking the comfort of familiarity
3. Being limited by what others deem age appropriate
4. Yielding to the inertia of procrastination
5. Tolerating toxic teasing
6. Pointing out personal flaws before others can point them out
7. Second-guessing others by assuming that they will respond negatively

Habit 1: Listening to Incompetent Others

As the cartoon about snakes needing legs to cross the street suggests, listening to others can have an effect on a person's beliefs and actions. When people listen to incompetent others before they take time to listen to themselves, they may be subjected to one of the tethers that make them a hostage to doubt.

Consider the last time you were asked to work with a group in a workshop and a self-appointed leader emerged by asserting herself and awing the group by tossing around a few key buzzwords. She was successful in overshadowing others and squelching hesitant information offerings from group members before other group members could view those remarks as credible and worthwhile. Such a person often has an effective command of language that gives others the mistaken impression that she is very knowledgeable.

The person who listens to everyone first and develops a credible argument or comment that is reflective of previous comments, prior knowledge, and personal experience usually makes the most useful contribution to a discussion. Careful thought and a planned response is far more valuable than the overzealous, impulsive remarks of a possibly less competent person vying to take over the group or impress others.

Functional paralysis is an affliction that besets many people who have to make a decision and then have difficulty making that decision because they fear the outcome. Some people so afflicted may ask the advice of many others, including incompetent others, to make those people whom they consult complicit in their decision making so that if it turns out to be a poor decision, someone else can share some or possibly all of the blame.

The cure for functional paralysis is courage of conviction, faith, or beliefs and trust that everything is as it is meant to be. With such conviction, there is no need to fear outcomes. Too much help seeking can foster a functional paralysis that compels a dependency, keeping a person from taking the initiative on an idea or engaging in informed risk taking. Asking for expert help is advised and encouraged for novice and veteran teachers when needed; however, listening to one knowledgeable voice is certainly better than listening to a chorus of voices of incompetent others.

Habit 2: Seeking the Comfort of Familiarity

People who have less faith in themselves tend to seek the comfort of the familiar and resist venturing out of their comfort zones. Many use terms like "I don't do that," "I wouldn't ever do that," or "I've never done that before, and I'm not likely to do it." Why not do it? That is the question. Why are they so risk averse that they refuse to try new ideas and activities?

One excuse that some people use is that they are too old or that they will look silly doing something if they can't do it perfectly. The necessary response is, So what if it is not perfect? It could be novel or innovative. One of the teachers in the survey wondered if she was too old to learn new things. Teachers don't have to be perfect—only effective. No one is too old to learn new tricks of the trade.

Brain research reveals that seniors who engage in cognitive challenges improve brain function. With proper nutrition, they can stave off cognitive impairment that accompanies deficiencies, such as that of vitamin D (Wilkins, Birge, Sheline, & Morris, 2009). Teachers can do the same and also entertain life challenges that force them out of their comfortable rut.

Unfortunately, when we think of venturing out to entertain an exciting, big idea, the tentacles of our resident doubts can wrap around our brains, snatch us back, and deposit us into our comfortable, negative-thinking rut. Positive self-efficacy can help a person break free of the tentacles of doubt and venture into the unknown to do great things.

Habit 3: Being Limited by What Others Deem Appropriate

Sometimes people seek order in their lives by thinking of neat mental boxes in which they place other people who have certain characteristics. These order seekers expect others whom they have relegated to these mental boxes to behave in a certain way at certain times and under certain circumstances. Order seekers may expect a new teacher with limited experience to work up to only a low level of limited experience and not stretch herself to try something requiring more knowledge and expertise than she may be thought to possess.

Some teachers believe that they are too old to learn the new technologies and consequently hold themselves and their students back when they try to avoid using new technology products. An older person may buy into what someone else deems age appropriate to avoid appearing foolish or inept. They doubt themselves and their ideas because they fail to consult the younger person who always remains inside all of us and who may not mind appearing foolish, especially if the reward is trying something new and different.

A little boy cried because he wanted to be the governor of New Jersey and everyone told him he was too small. This is a true story of a truly distraught child who resented being told that he was too small or that he had to wait to go to college before he could become governor. He refused to accept any of that rationale. His tearful despair was brought to the attention of the governor via broadcast and social media. His wish was granted when the governor of New Jersey made him honorary governor for a day (Family, 2011).

We can learn a lot from this child and reject the limitations others seek to put on us that make us doubt ourselves. Don't allow your plans of action to retreat to the recesses of your brain and dissipate into nothingness. To avoid the limitation of doing what others deem appropriate, periodically shake things up in your thinking and fluff out the crevices of your brain to dislodge ideas and dreams that are stuck in the cracks and need room to grow. Anything is possible if you consider the possibilities and encourage your students to do the same. Don't set limitations on your students; you never know what they might be capable of doing that is beyond what you and others might deem appropriate.

Habit 4: Succumbing to the Inertia of Procrastination

Procrastination is a form of doubt behavior. When people are unsure about a task and how to approach it, they may do the dance of procrastination, where they skirt the issue, examining it from all sides as they avoid taking action. A teacher could be on a fast roll thinking about a problem task, hit a pothole of doubt, and come to a screeching halt in her thinking. The resulting inertia of motion jerks her back into doubt mode, eroding any further action she might take on the problem—possibly forever.

There is a distinction between reflective evaluation of a task and procrastination; the former is a positive, temporary measure useful for planning. Procrastination may take longer, offering a crippling paralysis of thought that may keep the task from ever being completed. Procrastination manifests in a variety of forms: waiting for someone else to do the task first, endless gathering of data about the task, pointing out reasons a task cannot or should not be done, or listening to the inner voice that talks its host out of opportunities to accomplish something—to name only a few.

Recognizing when you're in procrastination mode is the first step toward loosening the grip of procrastination and moving forward and out of it. When you have said you are "gonna do" something 10 or more times and you haven't done what you said you are "gonna do," you're probably in procrastination mode and not likely to get it done.

The teacher who has said every year for the past six or so years that she is "going" to get parents more involved but has yet to do anything new that will make it happen may secretly doubt that she can make it happen or come up with a fail-proof strategy that will work. Until she comes up with something, she'll dance the dance of doubt and procrastination while chanting "I'm going do it, I'm going do it." Taking action is the only way to stop the music of doubt playing in your head, halt the dance of procrastination, muster up enough belief in yourself and your abilities to plunge head-on into the task, and trust that you will be resourceful and succeed.

The teacher who wants to get parents involved could resist the inertia of procrastination by announcing that she will have a student extravaganza in the spring to showcase her students and their accomplishments and that parents will be invited. She does not have to know all the details yet, but she can trust that she will know what to do when the time comes. Teachers should review their actions and procrastination responses periodically to see if they are due for a replacement or a tune-up; otherwise, they may wait on the sidelines of accomplishment, indefinitely, doubting that they will ever get back on track.

Habit 5: Enduring Toxic Teasing

Teasing can be good-natured fun or a cruel effort to hurt someone. There are many insecure people who try to make themselves feel better by seeking, finding, and exploiting any weaknesses they find in others. These perpetrators use their findings to label and brand people using comments such as "I'm not paying attention to anything you say, Greg, you are always looking for attention, always trying to impress someone," "Greg, you are not the creative type; we can do without your ideas," or "Greg, don't try any of your bright in your class; you'll only make it worse than it is; you screw up everything you touch." The sender delivers these vicious barbs in the context of joking or teasing.

Greg, however, does not perceive the remarks as a joke, but he feels powerless to defend himself lest he appear "thin-skinned" and unable to take a joke.

The perpetrator knows he has the upper hand because he can make Greg look and feel badly whether Greg speaks up or not. Perpetrators of teasing and their victims often have different interpretations of the teasing event, perpetrators perceiving the event as less damaging and more humorous than their victims perceive it (Kowalski, 2000). A cavalier attitude about toxic teasing may encourage the perpetrator to do it often.

Unfortunately for Greg, he may internalize the perpetrator's comments and start doubting himself. He may actually start to believe the comments because it helps him save face for enduring the teasing. Irrationally, he may rationalize that the teasing is probably true, so he should not be so perturbed when he hears the hurtful teases. But by ignoring the sender's hurtful teasing, he is nurturing the seeds of doubt planted by those toxic comments.

Most people would object if someone were to stab them with a sharp object and try to hurt them. Toxic teasing is like a psychological stab because it carries intangible barbs that tear deeply into a sensitive psyche, ripping and shredding self-esteem and self-confidence as it goes. No one has the right to inflict such barbs, and no one should ever have to endure them. When you sense that someone is playing the toxic teasing game with you, the only course of action is to stop it immediately. You can suppress the comments with civility to avoid appearing that you can't take a joke, such as "I'm sure you feel you are just joking or teasing, but I don't care for that type of teasing, and I prefer not to participate in it; if you mean no harm, then I don't expect to hear anymore teasing from you again. If however, I do hear it from you again, I will assume you are not joking and your intent is to hurt or disparage me" or "We can have fun without you using me as comedy fodder; tell me that joke about the reindeer again."

Such swift, straightforward dialogue communicates your concerns, feelings, and expectations in one fell swoop. There is no need to apologize for your honesty and courage as you deliver a heavy dose of reality to the teaser. You have a right to protect your belief in yourself and ward off any assaults that foster doubt regardless of the source.

Habit 6: Communicating Your Flaws to Others

Expectations often become self-fulfilling prophecies (Rosenthal & Jacobson, 1968). When people have low expectations for themselves and make it a habit of pointing out their flaws and communicating their self-doubt to others, they may cause others to also have low expectations of them. Consequently, they may doubt themselves enough to live up to those low expectations.

Teachers should refrain from self-disparagement of their teacher efficacy and from pointing out their flaws to others because they may rob themselves of a source of encouragement or empowerment that could help them succeed at a task. Sometimes, self-disparagement may be misconstrued as fishing for compliments, an act that may encourage the listener to agree with the negative remarks rather than be manipulated into giving a compliment. That unexpected agreement could foster self-doubt.

Habit 7: Assuming That Others Will Respond Negatively

A less direct means of communicating your flaws to others is answering for other people in the negative. This expectation that others may respond negatively to you is another form of self-sabotage that is fueled by self-doubt. A teacher who wants to use dance steps to teach a four-step math process may sabotage her idea by saying, "Oh, they won't want to do this; they'll think this is so silly." Second-guessing or assuming that you know what others think will derail your best intentions.

Have the courage to try your biggest and brightest ideas, expecting that they will be enlightening and effective. Know that as a highly effective teacher, you can successfully complete the challenges of teaching. When you ignite a contagious belief in yourself, you can expect that others will find you convincing and also believe in you.

QUIETING MIND CLUTTER WITH PROFESSIONAL ORGANIZATION

The quiet that is perceived and relished when surroundings are made orderly, particularly when they were previously in a state of disorganization and chaos, leads us to believe that there is a barely audible noise associated with clutter and chaos. This noise seems to manifest in the brain as a disconcerting buzz that stifles serenity, reflection, and opportunities for bold, productive thought. The serenity and calm of an orderly environment is more conducive to inspiring self-confidence than the bitter buzz of chaos because an orderly environment inspires a sense of control and command of oneself, contrary to the spiraling-out-of-control feeling induced by the instability and uncertainty of disorganization.

The mind becomes cluttered with fears of forgetting appointments or misplacing important documents, data, or materials and the endless stream of information committed to memory to avoid forgetting. There is also an accompanying sense of dread of being exposed as a disorganized person. This mind clutter provides a fertile environment for doubtful thoughts. If the brain is littered with the mind clutter of disorder, doubt can thrive because it will be difficult for self-confidence to reside and thrive in such an environment.

Disorder creeps into people's lives when they fail to respect the "physics" of organization, namely, remembering that what goes up must come down so that what is put down must be picked up. They fail to subscribe to the old adage "a place for everything and everything in its place," assuming that everything must have a place, or it doesn't belong and should be discarded or passed on to someone else. If the simple law of organization physics is violated continually, the end result is clutter and chaos.

Teachers can free their minds by maintaining an orderly environment. The confident, accomplished teacher most likely will have a clutter-free, highly organized classroom, and she probably has a maintenance plan to keep it that way. Organized teachers are somewhat deductive in their planning, beginning with the broad organizational needs and tailoring their classroom organization to the specific needs of themselves and students. They may outline general activities and assignments for the year and plan specifically for daily lesson plans and activities.

Detailed planning of lessons involves checklisting needed materials; correctly allocating the appropriate amount of time needed for assignments would address the concern of one of the survey teachers that she would not be able to manage her time. An additional concern was managing her student records. She also said, "I have always had a hard time keeping my records up to date and organized; I lived in fear of a spontaneous request for a student's record." Daily reconciliation of students' files would minimize her concern.

Culling or otherwise organizing student files that are in electronic folders or in traditional file folders and that are always in one place, such as a file drawer or file cabinet, would eliminate the concern of a spontaneous request for student records. It would also keep the teacher in compliance with the physics of classroom organization. Fear will be abated and replaced by self-confidence and a sense of empowered ability to respond to any request that relates to the classroom.

Professional organization of a classroom can be accomplished most effectively with a computer and a scanner. The latest scanning technology allows for scanning multiple documents quickly. The reduction of paper through scanning and electronic filing is a major step toward eliminating paper clutter. Organized teachers containerize classroom supplies and student materials and label or inventory them for ease of access. Having collection trays for student papers or electronic discussion boards keeps information centrally located and easily accessible. Consistency and regularity are the keys to keeping order. Teachers must sweep away the mind clutter of disorder and doubt as frequently as they would sweep away dust balls that hide under their furniture at home.

REFERENCES

Bandura, A. (1977). Self-efficacy: Toward a unifying theory of behavioral change. *Psychological Review, 84*(2), 191–215.

Family (Producer). (2011, April 2). Boy cries to be governor of New Jersey [video]. http://www.youtube.com/watch?v+qGuj-9jiCs4

Kowalski, R. (2000). "I was only kidding!": Victims' and perpetrators' perceptions of teasing. *Personality and Social Psychology Bulletin, 26*, 231–241.

Paulus, T., & Scherff, L. (2008). "Can anyone offer any words of encouragement?" Online dialogue as a support mechanism for preservice teachers. *Journal of Technology and Teacher Education, 16*(1), 113–136.

Rosenthal, R., & Jacobson, L. (1968). *Pygmalion in the classroom.* New York: Holt, Rhinehart and Winston.

Wilkins, C., Birge, S., Sheline, Y., & Morris, J. (2009). Vitamin D deficiency is associated with worse cognitive performance and lower bone density in older African Americans. *Journal of the National Medical Association, 101*(4), 349–354.

Woolfolk Hoy, A., Rosoff, B., & Hoy, W. K. (1990). Teacher's sense of efficacy and their beliefs about managing students. *Teaching and Teacher Education, 6*, 137–148.

Exercise 3.1: Are You a Hostage to Self-doubt??

Instructions: List ways that you can avoid the following 7 common habits that can tether your brain to self-doubts that can negatively affect you.

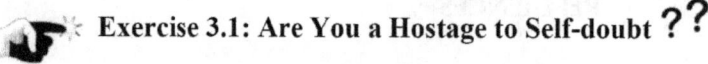

In what ways will you no longer listen to incompetent others or ask for advice before making a move??

_____
_____

In what ways will you no longer seek the comfort of familiarity to avoid uncertainty??

_____
_____

In what ways will you no longer allow your actions to be restricted by what others deem age-appropriate??

_____
_____

In what ways will you no longer yield to the inertia of procrastination??

_____
_____

In what ways will you no longer tolerate toxic teasing that causes you to doubt yourself??

_____
_____

In what ways will you no longer point out your personal flaws to keep others from pointing them out first??

_____
_____

In what ways will you no longer second-guess others by assuming they will respond negatively to you, your questions, or requests??

_____
_____

Exercise 3.2: Sweep Away Your Mind Clutter

Instructions: Which ones apply to you? Put an X beside them and tally up all points to see your state of mind clutter.

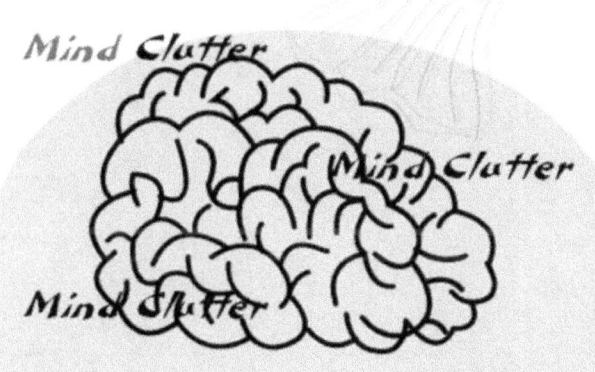

	You are always in a constant state of busyness.	10
	You often engage in nonproductive activity.	20
	You find many excuses for not completing a project.	20
	You allow trivia to intrude on your thought processes and interrupt your focus.	20
	You fear uncertainty and worry over the outcome.	10
	You refuse to use a calendar or planner.	20
	You sometimes ignore important tasks.	10
	You dance around a task, procrastinating.	10
	The pull of incomplete tasks occupies your brain space, blocking productive thoughts and creating pressure on you.	10
	Multitasking makes it difficult for you to focus on a task and finish something.	20
	You focus on the perceived drudgery or displeasure associated with the task making it difficult for you to start the task.	10
	You say yes to more tasks than you have time to complete.	20
	Total Points	
	0-40—Minor Clutter 50-90—Chronic Clutter 100-140—Chaotic Clutter 150-180—Crisis Clutter	

Phase II

RECONNECT: REPAIR AND RECONSTRUCT THE DAMAGE CAUSED BY NEGATIVE THOUGHTS

4

Getting a New Doubt-Averse Attitude
Replacing Fear with Trust

I've got a new attitude! No more moving in the slow lane for me.

To succeed we must first believe we can.

—Michael Korda

DENIAL: IT IS NOT A RIVER IN EGYPT (MARK TWAIN)

Walking into a room of many mirrors can be disconcerting for many people, especially if they are full-length mirrors. Mirrors tell undeniable truths that shatter illusions and personal deceptions. Human flaws are more perceptible and clear when viewed as mirror images. Lying to oneself has been a ploy used by many teachers to protect their tender egos and sense of well-being. Such lies protect from uncomfortable truths, but too many lies construct a reality that can no longer be trusted.

Teachers need to acknowledge when they are not teaching effectively, when they are no longer organized, when their classes are out of control, and when their children are not learning. To deny these truths is to negatively affect the learning of the students in their charge. Acknowledging personal shortcomings and flaws that have been previously hidden or disavowed actually provides teachers with a blueprint for betterment.

Teachers fear the vulnerability of disclosure because they are concerned about their reputations or what others might think of them. A renowned therapist says that having a strong sense of self is a necessary component of personal power and that denial is not a contributor to that power (McGraw, 2010). Effective teachers have to make sure they have clear perceptions of themselves that accurately reflect what is truly there.

Teachers who brag and brag about their competencies as teachers may, in fact, be covering up their inability to engage their students or manage discipline problems or some other masked area of weakness. Teachers who refuse to accept blame or constructive criticism or to admit that they made an error or that their lessons often fall flat engage in the most serious form of denial: self-deception.

The reality of self-deception is that it is a reality that can't be trusted. The psychological mirrors of the mind can reveal trustworthy truths that, if embraced and believed, will release the shackles of self-deception and deliver accurate perceptions of skills, flaws, and abilities. A liberated mind can improve one's metacognition and thereby help teachers know what they know, what they don't know, and what they need to know. The mirror exercise at the end of the chapter is useful for liberating truths from the mental reflection mirrors of the mind.

BOOSTING YOUR SELF-EFFICACY WITH A NEW ATTITUDE

A teacher's self-efficacy is her beliefs about her ability to promote students' learning that can be high, low, or somewhere in between; high self-efficacy is important for teacher success (Woolfolk & Hoy, 1990). Ross (1998) contends that highly efficacious teachers are open to new strategies and approaches that result in important learning outcomes for their students. A change in attitude can affect self-efficacy because stunted self-efficacy beliefs are rooted in old, ineffective attitudes, beliefs, and behaviors that are products of life experiences. It is possible to discard stagnated beliefs and attitudes and regrow new, fresh ones rooted in some of the good attitudes that remain.

Regrowing onions is a useful analogy for simulating a process of regrowing new attitudes and beliefs. Picture a large white onion; it typically has a short, dried, wilted stem at the top and some root hairs at the bottom. It has achieved its large size through new growth, layer by layer. For purposes of this analogy, the wilted stem represents old beliefs and attitudes. The layers represent years of experiences, good and bad, that influence those attitudes. The layers are the meat, or the substance, of the onion, much like a person's mental schema is the substance of the person. The roots represent possibilities for new growth.

The first step in boosting self-efficacy by regrowing a new attitude is to excise the old beliefs and attitudes that may be festering beneath self-doubts about one's abilities. This is like cutting off the dried, shriveled top of the onion. If the onion is cut in half and allowed to sit for weeks, amazingly, new robust stalks will grow out of the center of it, even without the presence of sunlight, water, or soil. The more substance or, in this case, good attitudes and beliefs there are left, the stronger and more vibrant the new emerging stalks (new attitudes and beliefs) will be.

A critical factor in the regrowth of new attitudes is identifying attitudes and beliefs that are not apparent. Burnout or emotional exhaustion is an enemy of teacher efficacy and can be minimized by avoiding being overwhelmed and overextended (Brouwers & Tomic, 2000). Many old beliefs foster teacher anger and frustration in the classroom. Power struggles abound where there should be peace, cooperation, and positive learning experiences. A new attitude will help teachers minimize or eradicate anger and frustration situations because they will have the self-efficacy to better deal with those problems and avoid any aberrant behavior and subsequent mistreatment of students.

Some of the old beliefs influencing teacher–pupil interactions involve controversies over punishment, such as when it should be used and how often, what types of punishment are appropriate, and the severity and frequency of use. Some teachers believe in severe punishment even for minor infractions. Some teachers believe in giving ultimatums, such as "Stop doing that, or you're going to the principal's office." Their lack of self-efficacy hinders their ability to draw on more effective alternatives to punishment because they tend to become frustrated easier when they feel somewhat powerless. Such teachers with poor self-efficacy may rely on others to compensate for their perceived lack of ability, engaging in actions such as sending students to the principal's office for minor disturbances and infractions that they should be able to handle.

A new attitude toward teacher–pupil interactions and altercations could help less efficacious teachers in all aspects of their professional development, such as professional skills, characteristics, strategies, approaches, motivation, and responses to student behavior. To improve their professional skills, teachers can opt to be more private with reprimands and discussions of student behaviors. As a result, privacy deescalates power struggles and is more empowering to low-efficacy teachers as they see they get better results. Learning better coping and classroom management skills will also improve attitudes.

Many teachers cite anger and frustration as the basic cause of their mistreatment of students (Orange, 2008). Day and Leitch (2001) say that knowing the role that teachers' emotions play in their professionalism is key to their understanding themselves. Managing frustration and avoiding mistakes can make a teacher feel more efficacious. Developing some of the following professional characteristics will help them have a positive influence on creating a new attitude:

- Be more respectful of students, such as exercising caution and prudence when discussing sensitive issues.
- Minimize blaming.
- Be more flexible; relax rules and practices when such an action would be more appropriate than punishment.
- Be less rigid, not having to have the last word or the upper hand; be open to help from others.
- Be less prone to act impulsively and make split-second decisions.
- Be more willing to change soft policies as the situation dictates (having such a mind-set is more likely to yield better outcomes).
- Be willing to apologize to students, without reservations, when the teacher is at fault.
- Be willing to share student problems with relevant others, such as counselors, parents, and administration, to get new perspectives on how to address those problems.
- Be willing to modify one's approach to a problem by evaluating a student's problematic behavior on a case-by-case basis, check circumstances before acting, and, most of all, follow the golden rule of "do unto others as you would have them do unto you."

Managing responses to student behavior is critical. To avoid the typical response of many teachers to frustration and anger, teachers should do the following:

- Be calm and temper displays of emotion with understanding and prudence.
- Breathe and allow for cool-down time to make better responses to adverse situations.
- Be careful and compassionate about what they say to students in the heat of anger.

- Never use grades as punishment.
- Resist the urge to utter the first words that come to them in an altercation with a student. They should take time to reflect on the student–teacher exchange and resist the urge to express anger.

Making positive changes in attitude will undoubtedly increase positive outcomes and teachers' beliefs that they can affect and obtain positive outcomes. A positive change in attitudes and beliefs provides teachers with the needed boost to more positive self-efficacy.

AVOID PROCRASTINATION: DON'T PUT OFF FOR TOMORROW WHAT YOU CAN DO TODAY

When embarking on a task, having a clear vision of the task and desired outcomes is an effective antidote for procrastination. Many teachers procrastinate at some point when facing a task that lacks certainty. Like most procrastinators, they dance around the task, stalling, deferring action, and entertaining distractions as they deftly find excuses for not starting the project. Procrastinators find themselves in a constant state of busyness: busy doing unimportant, irrelevant, nonproductive tasks.

The chronic avoider claims there are too many things to do and not enough time to do them and so does nothing, avoiding certain tasks and hoping they will go away. The pleasure-seeking procrastinator approaches a possibly difficult task with aversion, focusing on the perceived drudgery or unpleasantness associated with the task. The dreamer procrastinator allows trivia to flit in and out of one's thought processes, interrupting potentially productive thoughts and ideas. Finally, the anxious procrastinator is overwhelmed by the push and pull of uncompleted tasks, indecision, and inaction and merely frets and worries.

All of these models of procrastination fit Steel's (2007) conceptualization of procrastination as a self-regulatory failure and a failure to obey the wishes of the self. The underlying causes of this self-regulatory failure and lack of obedience to the self are many. Procrastination is often fueled by fear of negative outcomes and the uncertainty of outcomes. Too much uncertainty can feel like the possibility of pain, so people tend to avoid it (Pychyl, 2008). These emotions are so strong that they create inertia, crippling productivity. Procrastinators are often disorganized and late meeting or completing deadlines.

There are many consequences of procrastinating for teachers. Their lack of productivity can result in lower evaluations and poor teaching. The consequences of teacher procrastination subsequently have a negative effect on their students' grades and learning outcomes. Overcoming procrastination is not difficult. In fact, limiting procrastination is a way for teachers to decompress an overloaded brain, making room for organized creative thoughts and increased productivity. The following tips and strategies are useful for overcoming procrastination:

- Start with a list of tasks.
- Try not to put off any task for tomorrow that can be done today.
- If there are many tasks, categorize them.
- Ask others to help you brainstorm an idea if you feel stuck.
- Allocate adequate time before deadlines to complete your task.
- Break down the task into manageable subtasks and allocate the time needed for each subtask.
- Manage distractions.
- Become a self-regulation success; listen to your inner self and abstain from distracting behaviors no matter how pleasurable they may be.
- Defer pleasurable activities as a reward after task completion. This is referred to as "grandma's rule," where the privilege of participating in pleasurable activities is contingent on the completion of an undesirable task (Schunk, 2012).
- Use a planner; set a pre-deadline before the actual deadline to avoid being late.
- Prepare all materials needed before school starts. Store them electronically in folders, and they will be readily accessible.
- Become more aware of procrastinating behaviors. If there is a task that keeps getting put off, make a commitment to just do it and not commit to do anything else until it is done.

See the procrastination-busting strategies in exercise 4.3.

Why do people procrastinate? One of the simplest reasons people procrastinate is because they're unsure of what to do. Typically, people procrastinate because they prefer spending their time on a more desirable activity. For some people, the task may require more effort than the person is willing to give. If a person thinks the task is taxing or an energy drain, one may prefer to focus one's energies somewhere else that is less demanding.

When tasks appear onerous without a sufficiently rewarding outcome, people may procrastinate because they have doubts about being able to complete the task successfully. Some people hesitate when faced with choices; they procrastinate because they feel it is prudent to wait and investigate before acting in order to make the best choice. Indecision about what is needed to start the project or how to solve the problem promotes procrastination. Many people procrastinate when they perceive an inability to find the large allocation of time that may be needed to complete the project.

REFERENCES

Brouwers, A., & Tomic, W. (2000). A longitudinal study of teacher burnout and perceived self-efficacy in classroom management. *Teaching and Teacher Education, 16*(2), 239–253.

Day, C., & Leitch, R. (2001). Teachers' and teacher educators' lives: The role of emotion. *Teaching and Teacher Education, 17*(4), 403–415.

McGraw, P. (2010, October). Personal power: 6 rules for how to harness yours. *Oprah.com, 11,* 75–75.

Orange, C. (2008). *25 biggest mistakes teachers make and how to avoid them.* Thousand Oaks, CA: Corwin.

Pychyl, T. A. (2008, May 2). Delay as a self-handicapping strategy: I can protect my self-image by procrastinating? http://www.psychologytoday.com

Ross, J. (1998). *The antecedents and consequences of teacher efficacy* (Vol. 7). Greenwich, CT: JAI.

Schunk, D. H. (2012). *Learning theories: An educational perspective.* Upper Saddle River, NJ: Pearson/Merrill Prentice Hall.

Steel, P. (2007). The nature of procrastination: A meta-analytic and theoretical review of quintessential self-regulatory failure. *Psychological Bulletin, 133*(1), 65–94.

Woolfolk, A. E., & Hoy, W. K. (1990). Prospective teachers' sense of efficacy and beliefs about control. *Journal of Educational Psychology, 82*(1), 81–91.

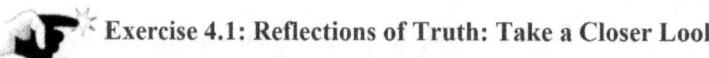
Exercise 4.1: Reflections of Truth: Take a Closer Look

Instructions: Fill in the blanks with perceptions of yourself as a teacher that you believe to be true. Get a mirror, look yourself in the eye and reflect on those perceptions for a few minutes. Ask yourself if the perception is true or untrue or only partially true. After careful thought, circle true, not true or partially true. Do not lie to yourself; be ruthlessly honest to discover new truths. If it is only true or partially true think hard about a new truth. Write your new truth on the line in the mirror that corresponds with the perception you are contemplating. An example of Perception #1 might be "I work as hard as I can." After reflection, the new truth is that you could work harder. The new truth is written on the line of truth #1 that corresponds with self-perception #1.

Self-Perception #1. I work as hard as I can _____True or Not True or Partially True?

Self-Perception #2. _____True or Not True or Partially True?

Self-Perception #3. _____True or Not True or Partially True?

Self-Perception #4. _____ True or Not True or Partially True?

Self-Perception #5. _____ True or Not True or Partially True?

Self-Perception #6. _____ True or Not True or Partially True?

I could work harder. _____ Truth #1.   Truth #2. _____

_____ Truth #3.   Truth #4. _____

_____ Truth #5.   Truth #6. _____

 **Exercise 4.2: Check Your "Self-Efficacy"**

Instructions: Put a check mark in the box ☑ under the appropriate response, as it applies to you, for each statement. Tally your responses in each category of never, rarely, maybe, often, and always and put the total in the self-efficacy score box. Find your score interpretation under Self-Efficacy Interpretations. Refer to this chart as a reminder to change your attitudes and boost your score where needed.

Beliefs	Never	Rarely	Maybe	Often	Always
I am confident of my ability to achieve my goals.					
I tend to persevere when I encounter adversity.					
I believe I am capable of achieving anything I try.					
I inspire confidence in myself and my students.					
I refuse to entertain negative self-talk because I can do it.					
I can skillfully generate and organize ideas.					
I can overcome setbacks and keep going until I succeed.					
I defeat self-doubt with preparation.					
I trust my instincts to make good decisions.					
I can efficiently learn new skills.					
I am willing to leave my comfort zone to try new ideas.					
I positively affirm myself when I'm working through problems.					
I know a variety of effective problem solving strategies.					
I have the perseverance to see things through.					
I affirm my self-efficacy by correcting and avoiding mistakes.					
I fully use all of my talents when challenged by problems.					
I believe I have more strengths than weaknesses.					
I usually feel optimistic about successfully completing tasks.					
I am very competent in most areas of my life.					
When I tackle a new problem, I believe I will be successful.					

	Number of responses in each category	Points for each response	Subtotal of each category
Always		X 5	=
Often		X 4	=
Sometimes		X 3	=
Rarely		X 2	=
Never		X 0	=
		Total	

Self-Efficacy Score Interpretations

High Self-Efficacy	Score: 100-80
Moderate Self-Efficacy	Score: 79-60
Low Self-Efficacy	Score: 59-below

Exercise 4.3: Procrastination-Busting Strategies to Get You on a Roll

Instructions: Give an example of how you can use each strategy.

Cinnamon Swirl Roll—Move forward with deliberation, not hesitation, and expand your ideas in many directions. Ex. _____	Bagel—Slice through difficult problems with well-planned solutions to avoid procrastinating. Ex. _____
Sweet Roll—Don't hesitate to try new pedagogies; success is a sweet deal. Ex. _____	Doughnut—Close the "holes" in your classroom policies and teaching practices that invite procrastination. Ex. _____
Hoagie Roll—Develop a Broad Spectrum of Knowledge to avoid procrastinating. Ex. _____	Brown and Serve Rolls—Don't hesitate to be quick-thinking in uncertain situations. Ex. _____
Crescent Roll—Wrap-up your lessons with a review of what was learned and what to expect next time, to avoid procrastinating. Ex. _____	Pull-Apart Roll—Segment your problem into manageable parts to make it easier to solve the problem and avoid hesitation. Ex. _____
Dollar Roll—The price of indecision is too high; make a decision, take action, and roll with the outcomes. Ex. _____	Pretzel Roll—Don't get tied up in knots and avoid putting things off. Ex. _____

5

Jump-Starting Your Teacher Efficacy

I figured out that if I want to make it to the top of my profession, I have to change direction.

Whether you think you can or think you can't, you're right.

—Henry Ford

USING BEST TEACHING PRACTICES AND RESEARCH-TESTED TEACHING STRATEGIES

What teaching methods are most effective? The answer to that question continues to intrigue educators. They want to employ the best teaching practices, that is, the most effective, measurable results that can be delivered using reliable, tested teaching strategies. For example, using the reading method that is most likely to produce the best results, best practices make teachers feel more effective because the teaching techniques employed have been researched, tested, analyzed, and approved or recommended.

Research-based or evidence-based teaching (Petty, 2014) improves the likelihood of successful teaching outcomes. When teachers are knowledgeable about best practices in teaching, they are likely to feel more competent and confident, thereby jump-starting their teacher efficacy, or their beliefs in their ability to positively affect student learning outcomes. Teacher efficacy also includes teachers' beliefs in their abilities to organize and execute courses of action necessary to bring about desired learning outcomes (Woolfolk & Hoy, 1990).

An early reading practice, using the whole-word or the sight-word approach, was epitomized in the *Dick and Jane* graded basal readers (Gray & Sharp, 1930). The whole-word approach focused on teaching vocabulary as sight words by exposing students to new whole words, such as "Look, look, Jane," repeatedly in special stories that included some phonetic analysis. The answer to this question has long been the subject of much debate spawning the "reading wars," or the dispute over which is the best way to teach reading—phonics or whole-language approaches (the latter not to be confused with the whole-word approach).

Research has shown that phonics, an approach to teaching reading that emphasizes the sound/symbol relationship in alphabetic writing, may have some advantages over whole language. However, the use of both strategies together—phonics instruction and other reading instruction—may be most effective for teaching students how to read (Reyhner, 2008).

Teachers want to use the best strategies for gaining students' attention, motivating and engaging them to learn the material, assessing their progress, and fostering their retention of the subject matter.

Evidence-based teaching strategies are available for most subjects. Having knowledge of timely, proven strategies will help teachers improve and believe in their capabilities as teachers, also known as teacher efficacy. The use of strategies that will have the greatest effect on student achievement will help teachers jump-start their teacher efficacy because they can be more assured that they are doing their best job of teaching. They will experience less doubt because research results offer some evidence of the effectiveness of their teaching strategies that should ultimately improve the quality of the teaching.

LEARNING THEORIES MEDIATE BEST PRACTICES

Much best practices research reflects learning theories that answer the "why" of teaching to avoid educational tasks that are only busywork. Some of the more well known theories of learning include behaviorism, social cognitive learning theory, information processing, and theories of motivation, constructivism, and cognitivism. These theories can be seen in action in most classrooms at some point in time.

From behaviorism, we see token economies, where children receive rewards for positive behaviors and receive punishment for undesirable behaviors. Social cognitive learning is useful for understanding bullying behavior or the teaching of prosocial behaviors. Cognitive learning theory offers a concept attainment model that explains how students learn concepts. Information processing explains the "why" and "how" of the importance of getting student attention before trying to teach, especially if the desired outcome is that the student perceives the meaning of the information, retains the information in long-term memory, and is able to retrieve it at will.

Constructivism, a learning theory developed by Piaget and Vygotsky (Powell & Kalina, 2009), emphasizes that learners develop meaning by relating new knowledge to their previous knowledge. In constructivist teaching, teachers provide hands-on, or experiential, opportunities for students to discover meaning for themselves. Research-based teaching has a theoretical framework that provides background information for the practice that is being tested or assessed. This research is most likely rooted in some form of learning theory. Much of the research is useful for determining which practices are better than others.

Having a theoretical basis for best practices enables the teacher to be flexible in the application of the practice in a variety of appropriate settings and to accommodate student differences under various learning conditions. A selection of useful, enduring best practices in the areas of student development, effective teacher–pupil interactions, essential teaching strategies, discipline, teaching, and learning is listed below. With frequent use, the best practices featured here will give doubtful teachers an appreciative boost in efficacy and encourage better teaching.

Student Development

- Increase efforts to help students improve their *self-efficacy beliefs* and perceptions of their ability to accomplish certain tasks (Bandura, 1993); decrease unnecessary criticism of their efforts.
- Increase efforts to prepare *developmentally appropriate instruction* and assessment. Be aware of limitations of students' cognitive development and increase efforts to match educational tasks with students' thinking and abilities (Piaget, 1958; Kostelnik, Gregory, Soderman, & Whiren, 2011); avoid assigning tasks beyond students' current cognitive capabilities.

- Increase efforts to display a *humanistic teaching attitude* toward economically at-risk students and help them satisfy their deficiency needs if possible (Maslow, 1968); decrease efforts that expect them to be concerned with growth needs if they currently have deficiency needs.
- Increase efforts to promote students' *self-esteem* and feelings about their self-worth, earned recognition, and praise (Leary, Tambor, Terdal, & Downs, 1995); avoid disparaging, nonconstructive feedback and undeserved praise.
- Use *ability grouping* for specialized tasks to remediate groups as needed based on their performance and skills in light of the subject being taught (Harringan, Rosenthal, & Scherer, 2005); avoid ability grouping as a general practice.
- Use low-arousal teaching strategies in complex testing situations (Diamond, 2005; Yerkes & Dodson, 1908); avoid high-stress/high-arousal strategies in complex test situations to minimize *test anxiety*.
- Increase efforts to help students learn to appropriately attribute their successes and failures (Weiner, 1985); help discourage their use of blaming good or bad luck for their failures or successes.

Effective Teacher–Pupil Interactions

- Increase the use of assessments that are fair and exercise fairness in creating relevant assessments (Popham, 2011); avoid assessments with apparent *test bias*.
- Increase the effective use of *praise* and be clear and systematic about the behavior that is being praised (Dweck, 2007); decrease the use of punishment (praise is more effective than punishment).
- For better learning outcomes, increase time given to students to think before asking for the answer (Tobin, 1987); avoid shorter *wait times* for girls.
- Increase efforts to communicate your positive beliefs in students' abilities, and those beliefs will be more likely to become *self-fulfilling prophecies* (Rosenthal & Jacobson, 1968); decrease communication of a lack of belief in students' abilities and criticisms, which can also become self-fulfilling prophecies.
- Increase effective instruction that lies somewhere between a child's current level of development and his or her ability to solve problems and what the child can achieve with adult assistance or capable peer assistance, known as the *zone of proximal development* (Vygotsky, 1978); be aware of the zone of proximal development when assisting students and gradually decrease their need for assistance using scaffolding.

Essential Teaching Strategies

- Establish relevant *behavioral objectives* by stating the objectives first in general terms and giving pertinent examples (Gronlund, 1969); avoid activities that don't have relevant objectives, as they are ineffective.
- Increase the use of *authentic classroom assessments* that are as reliable and valid as possible and improve student performance with useful feedback (Wiggins, 1993); avoid assessments that are simply audits of performance.
- Increase the use of *allocated time* for maximum *student engagement* (Woolfolk, 2013); decrease distractions and interruptions.
- Increase the use of *culturally responsive teaching* strategies to make learning more personally interesting and appealing to accommodate student diversity (Gay, 2010); decrease the use of knowledge and content that is less relevant and accommodating to student diversity.
- Increase efforts to use *differentiated instruction* or multilevel lessons to match appropriate teaching methods and *individualized instruction* with the current levels of knowledge, skills, and abilities of students (Tomlinson, 1999); decrease teaching efforts that use a one-size-fits-all approach.

Positive Discipline

- Increase the use of behavior management strategies to redirect inappropriate student behavior, encourage students to rethink bad behavior, and praise good behavior (Hayes, 2012; Skinner, 1965); decrease the use of external rewards, ignore minor inappropriate behaviors, and make punishment a last resort.

Learning

- Promote effective learning using *brain-based learning* and teaching strategies that employ neuroscience to inform instruction and enhance students' learning (Sousa, 2011); to enhance learning, decrease the use of teaching strategies that ignore the way the brain works.
- Offer reasonable challenges to students using *discovery learning* or inquiry assignments that are teacher-facilitated discovery, yielding the most optimal outcome (Bruner, 1961); avoid teacher-dominated discovery learning assignments that are suboptimal.
- Increase opportunities for students to participate in self-directed learning and encourage them to become *self-regulated learners* (Schunk & Zimmerman, 1998); decrease teacher-centered direct instruction whenever possible.

- Develop *problem-based learning* strategies; increase the use of problem-based learning methods (Savin-Baden & Wilkie, 2006); decrease the use of traditional methods, such as lecture and other static methods.

SOLVING THE MYSTERY OF GETTING GREAT TEACHER EVALUATIONS

Teacher evaluations are the most potent source of fear and doubt in the educational process. When an authority figure, such as an administrator, is empowered to judge a teacher's performance, the anticipation of that judgment can elicit fear and anxiety because the outcome carries a lot of weight for the teacher being evaluated. Many people have a high degree of fear of evaluation because the outcome may be unfavorable.

For some teachers, a negative rating validates existing feelings of inadequacy and encourages a retreat within oneself to nurture the doubts residing there. Also, some teachers are fearful that others may believe the administrator's negative assessment regardless of how inaccurate it may be. Fortunately for some teachers, a negative rating is a call to action and a willingness to make positive changes.

For others, it may be a source of shame and doubt about whether they can make positive changes. Worse yet, the outcome may be dismissal and loss of livelihood. The effects of negative evaluations are compounded because teachers are often negatively portrayed in media and blamed for almost all of society's ills but mostly for the low academic performance of America's children, especially when compared to children in other countries.

Classrooms, by nature, are dynamic, interactive, and multidimensional, meaning the teacher must juggle many students, multiple tasks, responsibilities, and time constraints (Woolfolk, 2013). The moment a teacher steps into a classroom, it's as if there were a great number of balls in the air and she has to catch them all and keep them in motion without dropping any of them. Unlike the skillful circus juggler who has to keep the ball in play for only a brief period of time, the teacher has to do it 6 to 7 hours a day, every day, during the school year.

In addition, frequent unexpected balls of classroom interactions are thrown in, and she has to adjust her rhythm to accommodate new balls, such as disruptions, interruptions, parent visits, administrative requests, and so on. It's understandable that teachers may have doubts about their ability to handle the multidimensionality of classroom management. To appropriately address the complex interactions and expected outcomes associated with teacher evaluations, it is necessary to identify or classify dimensions of classroom teaching and concerns and doubts and to research best practices to inform solutions.

Use hindsight to your advantage by evaluating your lessons and giving yourself feedback. Make changes to your approach to teaching based on that feedback, observe master teachers, and seek help refining your new instructional processes. You should try to avoid situations that foster doubt. For example, if you are teaching out of your discipline, evaluation may be stressful. To be successful in this type of situation, muster up the courage to ask someone who has credentials in the discipline and who has been teaching in that discipline to clarify areas that you don't understand; pride and ego are luxuries that you can't afford.

If your teacher preparation pathway is different from traditional education, such as changing careers and participating in a fast-track teaching program, you may have missed some of the teaching strategies because of the time constraints of the program. In such cases, it's prudent and appropriate to contact professors at the university that sponsored the teaching program and ask for help. Commit your new strategies to memory as a plan of action and then create a checklist to guide your actions, collect evidence of your success and professional development, and set up a file for organizing that evidence.

What are teaching evaluations? We may define them as a set of criteria designed to comprehensively measure the competencies of teachers within the context of a set of educational standards. Nationally, there are numerous problems associated with teacher evaluations, such as having no established criteria or consensus on standards. The nature of teaching is such that it is difficult to fairly evaluate a year of teaching with one or two observations. The teacher evaluation system is admittedly flawed; however, evaluations are an important part of the American educational process because most administrators believe that evaluations make better teachers.

Teaching evaluations are a fact of life and are here to stay, so it is best to prepare for them. Prior to scheduled evaluations, teachers should make every effort to establish rapport with the current administration before evaluation. Yes, that means trying to make them like you. A high school student once commented that he always tried to make his teachers like him because if they liked him, they wouldn't want to hurt him. Having someone like you opens the door for mutual respect and understanding—important elements of rapport. Teachers should make it a practice to seek help when needed or to ask the administration about their expectations and areas of concern.

Asking the administration about their concerns and problems with faculty performance gives you some insight into which professional behaviors you should perfect and which unprofessional behaviors you should avoid. You want to gain administrators' respect and friendship because of your talents and abilities, not because of a special personal relationship that could sour and affect future professional interactions and evaluations. Professionalism is preferable to favoritism.

All teachers should have a professional library that they consult on a regular basis for tips on teaching strategies, effective pedagogy, activities for better student engagement, and any other techniques or tactics that will improve teaching. Consult publishers' websites for books that would be helpful in your efforts to improve your teaching. Other areas of preparation might involve asking colleagues to informally evaluate your teaching. Self-evaluation is also an effective means of critiquing your teaching.

Videotaping a lesson as you teach will give you the necessary information to make an informed appraisal of your teaching. If you want more objective feedback, volunteer to set up a professional development workshop for your peers on professional development day and present the following reflection exercise.

Reflection Exercise 1: Peer Assessment of Teaching

Teachers who agree to participate will teach a mini-lesson to the group that will be videotaped. The group will anonymously critique the mini-lesson based on a set of agreed-on criteria. The critiques will be collected and put into an envelope with the appropriate teacher's name on it. Each teacher should receive a copy of the videotape of their lesson and an opportunity to view it privately as they read the critiques.

Breakout rooms are perfect for this type of activity. When those teachers reconvene, they may share reactions to their critique and any strategies they may have for improving their teaching as a result of the exercise. Constructive criticism from participants should be delivered in a professional, helpful manner.

As you constructively critique your teaching, avoid disparagement; too much criticism can be depressing and halt positive action. Remember that the bottom line is improved student achievement, not discouragement. Use the critique of your peers and your critique of your own teaching to help you prepare your teaching objectives for the school year. Don't choose a subject that you are unfamiliar with or that you have had trouble with in the past for the lesson that you plan to have evaluated, that is, assuming you have the option of choosing the lesson that you want evaluated.

You should continuously add to your repertoire of basic teaching skills that are necessary for handling any type of educational problem. You should also brainstorm activities that will help you develop in the various areas of teaching, particularly the subject matter that you teach. Plan, plan, and then plan some more.

The key to having great teacher evaluations is not a big secret; it is simply discovering the right things to do and then doing them right. How do you discover the right things to do? The Internet is an invaluable resource for teaching techniques, teaching resources, and information on effective teaching. A step-by-step approach might involve first creating several broad categories that pertain to various aspects of teaching.

Those categories might include classroom management, understanding learners, student achievement, interpersonal skills, understanding the teaching environment, teaching strategies, and so on. Compiling a list of teacher competencies from your school district and other school districts will also inform you of the right things to do to be a great teacher. Examples of competencies involved in understanding learners are the following:

- The teacher uses an understanding of child development to create developmentally appropriate instruction.
- The teacher creates a classroom environment that promotes diversity and celebrates the individual student.
- The teacher is committed to fostering positive student self-concept and self-esteem.
- The teacher understands how to motivate and promote student learning.
- The teacher encourages reflective and critical thinking.
- The teacher uses a variety of media to communicate ideas and concepts in lessons.
- The teacher uses a variety of materials and resources to accommodate learning styles of all students.

Next, create a self-evaluation checklist by drawing three columns. In the first column, use your broad categories as labels. In the next two columns, put your assessment of your teaching: label the second column "I meet standards" and the third column "I don't meet standards." List all the competencies that you have collected and check whether you do or do not meet standards. Where there are a number of checks in the "I don't meet standards column," it may be prudent to add action strategies for meeting teaching standards.

Begin by embracing the attitude that an evaluation is an opportunity to showcase your talents as a teacher. Brainstorm ideas for a spectacular lesson with some of your colleagues and invite constructive suggestions. Create the most professional-looking materials possible. Be sure to include your students' ideas and suggestions for better lessons and for making your teaching more learner-centered. Make the subject matter informative, interesting, current, and relevant; do some research if necessary.

Don't be afraid to make your scheduled lesson observation a "dog and pony show," meaning outstanding in all aspects. Review the content of your lesson and rehearse your presentation of the information. In other words, it is "showtime," so show off. To improve the probability of getting great teacher evaluations, it is necessary to collect evidence of your accomplishments throughout the school year to present to your evaluator. Use the exercise for teacher evaluations (see exercise 5.2, parts I, II, and III) to list some possible samples of evidence.

You should begin saving evidence at the beginning of the school year. Prepare a self-statement of your teaching performance and include documents, artifacts, certificates, and so on as evidence that will be useful for giving administrators a broader picture of your teaching performance. In summary, the steps to a great teacher evaluation are the following:

Development—Assembling a broad set of teaching categories.
Implementation—Employing multiple research-based teaching strategies in your lesson.
Preparation—Planning a super, fantastic "dog and pony show" lesson for administrators to observe.
Presentation—Captivating your evaluator using multimedia, artifacts, displays, or other methods of making your lessons stand out.
Documentation—Collecting samples of student records, materials developed, notes from parents and students, teaching awards, sample lesson plans, and everything you do that could possibly be evaluated; these samples are evidence.

Teaching a spectacular lesson and receiving positive feedback from administrators, students, or other teachers may inspire you to teach your lessons this way whenever possible. Remember that the key to great teacher evaluations is to find out the right things to do and do them right—as often as possible. If you receive a poor evaluation, what should you do, assuming it is not your last chance? You can ask the evaluator to help you develop an action or improvement plan. In this plan, address areas that need improvement as identified by the evaluator and areas that you realized were weak during your teaching of the lesson.

Encourage your evaluator to help you set some objectives for your next evaluation. Both of you should agree on the objectives. Having objectives eliminates much of the uncertainty and gives you guidelines for what you need to do to be successful next time. If you meet your objectives and your lesson is spectacular, you have increased the odds of getting a great evaluation.

You also should tell the evaluator what you need and expect from the administration to help you be successful. If you received a poor evaluation, never be rude, defensive, or insubordinate. Remain cordial and cooperative and continue to participate lest you marginalize yourself and set yourself up for a biased view of your next teaching evaluation, which may be clouded by any residual, resentful responses from you. Focus on doing more better and faster and get great teaching evaluations.

MANAGING THE UNCERTAINTIES OF TEACHING

It is such irony that perceptions of teaching are often synonymous with perceptions of certainty because teachers are supposed to know all the answers and be almost everything to all students. The irony is that uncertainty is implicit in almost every area of teaching. Helsing (2007) suggests that uncertainty is an inherent feature of teaching. In reality, many teachers are laden with indecision, trepidation, misgivings, and other trappings of uncertainty because they doubt their efficacy or ability to effect desirable student outcomes. There is no way that teachers will know all the answers and be all things to all children; teachers are aware of that, and many of them express their feelings about it as self-doubt.

Some teachers believe the hype that teachers are supposed to be all-knowing and subsequently don a mantle of perfectionism that strains the fabric of their teaching efforts. Others can accept that certainty is not a trait they possess, and they are willing to accept resourcefulness as a plausible substitute. Helsing (2007) further suggests that teachers should respond to the uncertainties of teaching with experimentation and creativity within the context of their work setting. Both perfectionist and nonperfectionist teachers can learn to be flexible and creative as they manage uncertainty if they have a good risk management plan.

Uncertainty in teaching is usually associated with some threat or risk to a teacher's job, reputation, career, status, or tenure. There are many sources of risk in the classroom that foster uncertainty, such as the following:

- The classroom configuration is not conducive to optimal learning.
- Seating invites discipline problems.
- Hazardous materials are present, such as in science labs.
- Teachers are forced to teach a subject or grade outside of their discipline.
- An urgent request for students' work is made, or records are not well organized.
- Student injuries result from classroom items or other students.
- Unruly students are difficult to control.
- Coworkers are difficult to work with.
- A surprise teacher evaluation is given.
- Demanding parents make unexpected or unscheduled visits.
- Less-than-effective administration makes unreasonable demands.

Teachers may feel the need to manage the risk of poor reflections on their teaching performance, learning outcomes, or relationships with administration and coworkers. Teaching is an enterprise much like a business. A business enterprise typically seeks to minimize risk and maximize positive outcomes. To manage risk, business owners try to minimize and control critical variables, such as expenses, location, types of products, prices, skilled employees, and so on.

Teachers need to manage variables such as allocated learning time, condition of facilities, parent involvement, student skill levels, student motivation, and classroom appearance. Risk has a negative connotation, but it is not always bad. Positive change has some inherent risk, and change should be embraced and not seen as a negative that needs to be eliminated. Teacher doubt and subsequent guilt feelings about it may foster a desire for learning and meaningful improvements (Wheatley, 2002).

Accepting such risk may result in new and exciting outcomes that may not have materialized or come to fruition if the risk was minimized or eliminated. To minimize risk, teachers should try to anticipate problems that have occurred in various settings in the past and that are likely to happen again and plan an intervention to prevent a recurrence. The reaction to uncertainty is often self-doubt, which undermines teachers' confidence and efficacy.

Some teachers are concerned about the effectiveness of their teaching and whether the students understand the content. They're concerned about the appropriateness of their teaching. Some teachers are concerned about their lack of understanding or knowledge of child development and difficult material. They struggle to determine the best learning outcomes and making good instructional decisions that are appropriate strategies for dealing with uncertainty.

Teachers can practice doing "what-ifs" by mentally picturing the subsequent domino effect of their actions and possible outcomes that may be undesirable to allow themselves the opportunity to circumvent or avoid mistakes or risk. Teachers can maximize the positive effects of trial-and-error learning, keeping in mind that what works well with one group of students might not work well with another.

Teachers can make an inventory of their sources of uncertainty and determine if it is controllable or uncontrollable (Weiner, 1985). For example, a controllable source of uncertainty is feeling inadequate, lacking the skills or knowledge of difficult material, as there are numerous resources on the Internet that can help teachers build skills and increase their efficacy and competence.

An example of an uncontrollable source of uncertainty is the number and type of students who will be enrolled in the class. In most cases, teachers have little control over the students who will be enrolled in their class, so a positive response is to take action to control circumstances that can be changed and ignoring or accepting circumstances that cannot be changed, such as student enrollment.

Fear of making a mistake and the consequent hesitation to act is a poor response to uncertainty. Accepting the possibility of a mistake by working to minimize the possible negative repercussions is a more productive strategy. Uncertainty associated with always needing to have the right answers should be more about having a good response to uncertainty, such as telling the truth—saying, "I don't know, but I'll find out."

Teachers should accept that they may not always have the right answer or a ready response and be willing to use the Internet or reference books to find the correct answer while saying, "I'm not sure about that, and I don't want to give some incorrect information, so let's look it up and see." Teachers can be hopeful when accepting that managing uncertainty gets better with experience. The only absolute certainty about teaching is that it has many areas of uncertainty, such as levels of teacher knowledge, sophistication of teaching approaches, school climate, socioeconomic status of the student body, and so on.

Teachers should take refresher courses and seek help from experienced teachers when necessary to minimize the potential effects of uncertainty. Self-evaluation can help teachers develop sensors that become good predictors of what is effective and ineffective about a particular lesson. If there's concern about whether students are learning the information being taught, a variety of assessments may provide more comprehensive and better indicators of student understanding.

When using assessments to determine the effectiveness of teaching or student learning, remember that uncontrollable variables may confound the results, such as the student's home situation, which may preclude getting adequate sleep or nutrition—both of which can influence assessment outcomes. Assessment results are interpreted better as indicators than as absolutes.

Additionally, the quality of questioning can provide some insight into the effectiveness of teaching and quality of learning outcomes. Asking students, "Does everyone understand? Are there any questions?" usually begets the proverbial blank stare in silence as a response. Having students raise their hands to signal that they don't understand can also be ineffective. To avoid this phenomenon, ask for everyone who understands to raise their hands. Astute teachers can develop their own codes or signals that provide anonymity, such as discrete hand signals (a finger on the nose or two fingers on the chest) to let the teacher know that they don't understand or that they would like to have something repeated.

REFERENCES

Bandura, A. (1993). Perceived self-efficacy in cognitive development and functioning. *Educational Psychologist*, *28*(2), 117–148.

Bruner, J. S. (1961). The act of discovery. *Harvard Educational Review*, *31*, 21–32.

Diamond, D. M. (2005). Cognitive, endocrine and mechanistic perspectives on non-linear relationships between arousal and brain function. *Nonlinearity in Biology, Toxicology, and Medicine*, *3*(1), 1–7.

Dweck, C. (2007). The perils and promises of praise. *Educational Leadership: Early Intervention at Every Age*, *65*(2), 34–39.

Gay, G. (2010). *Culturally responsive teaching: Theory, research, and practice*. New York: Teachers College Press.

Gray, W., & Sharp, Z. (1930). *Dick and Jane*. Chicago: Scott Foresman.

Gronlund, N. E. (1969). *Stating behavioral objectives for classroom instruction.* New York: Macmillan.

Harrigan, J. A., Rosenthal, R., & Scherer, L. R. (Eds.). (2005). *The new handbook of methods in nonverbal behavior research.* New York: Oxford University Press.

Hayes, N. M. (2012). *Behavior management: Traditional and expanded approaches.* Lanham, MD: University Press of America.

Helsing, D. (2007). Regarding uncertainty in teachers and teaching. *Teaching and Teacher Education, 23*(8), 1317–1333.

Kostelnik, M., Gregory, K., Soderman, A., & Whiren, A. (2011). *Guiding children's social development and learning.* California: Wadsworth Cengage Learning.

Leary, M. R., Tambor, E. S., Terdal, S. K., & Downs, D. L. (1995). Self-esteem as an interpersonal monitor: The sociometer hypothesis. *Journal of Personality and Social Psychology, 68*(3), 518–530.

Maslow, A. H. (1968). *Toward a psychology of being.* New York: Wiley.

Petty, G. (2014). *Evidence-based teaching: A practical approach* (2nd ed.). Oxford: Oxford University Press.

Popham, J. (2011). *Classroom assessment: What teachers need to know* (6th ed.). Boston: Pearson Education.

Powell, K. C., & Kalina, C. J. (2009). Cognitive and social constructivism: Developing tools for an effective classroom. *Educational and Psychological Measurement, 130*(2), 241–250.

Reyhner, J. (2008). The reading wars: Phonics versus whole language.

Rosenthal, R., & Jacobson, L. (1968). Pygmalion in the classroom. *The Urban Review, 3*(1), 16–20.

Savin-Baden, M., & Wilkie, K. (2006). *Problem-based learning online.* London: McGraw-Hill Education.

Schunk, D. H., & Zimmerman, B. J. (1998). *Self-regulated learning—From teaching to self-reflective practice.* New York: Guilford.

Skinner, B. F. (1965). *Science and human behavior.* New York: Free Press.

Sousa, D. A. (2011). *How the brain learns.* Thousand Oaks, CA: Corwin.

Tobin, K. (1987). The role of wait time in higher cognitive level learning. *Review of Educational Research, 57*(1), 69–95.

Tomlinson, C. A. (1999). *The differentiated classroom: Responding to the needs of all learners.* Alexandria, VA: Association for Supervision and Curriculum Development.

Vygotsky, L. S. (1978). *Mind in society: The development of high psychological processes.* Cambridge, MA: Harvard University Press.

Weiner, B. (1985). An attributional theory of achievement motivation and emotion. *Psychological Review, 92*(4), 548–573.

Wheatley, K. F. (2002). The potential benefits of teacher efficacy doubts for educational reform. *Teaching and Teacher Education, 18*(1), 5–22.

Wiggins, G. P. (1993). *Assessing student performance.* San Francisco: Jossey-Bass.

Woolfolk, A. E. (2013). *Educational psychology* (12th ed.). Boston: Pearson Education.

Woolfolk, A. E., & Hoy, W. K. (1990). Prospective teachers' sense of efficacy and beliefs about control. *Journal of Educational Psychology, 82*(1), 81–91.

Yerkes, R. M., & Dodson, J. D. (1908). The relation of strength of stimulus to rapidity of habit-formation. *Journal of Comparative Neurology and Psychology, 18*, 459–482.

Exercise 5.1: Piecing Together Best Practices for Better Teaching

Instructions: Solve the puzzle by using a colored pen to substitute letters for the underlined spaces to reveal words related to Best Practices mentioned in the previous reading. The answers will be at the end of chapter 5. SCORING KEY: 13-11 correct = excellent; 10-9 correct = very good; 8-7 correct = good; 6-0 correct = needs improvement, seek additional exposure to Best Practices.

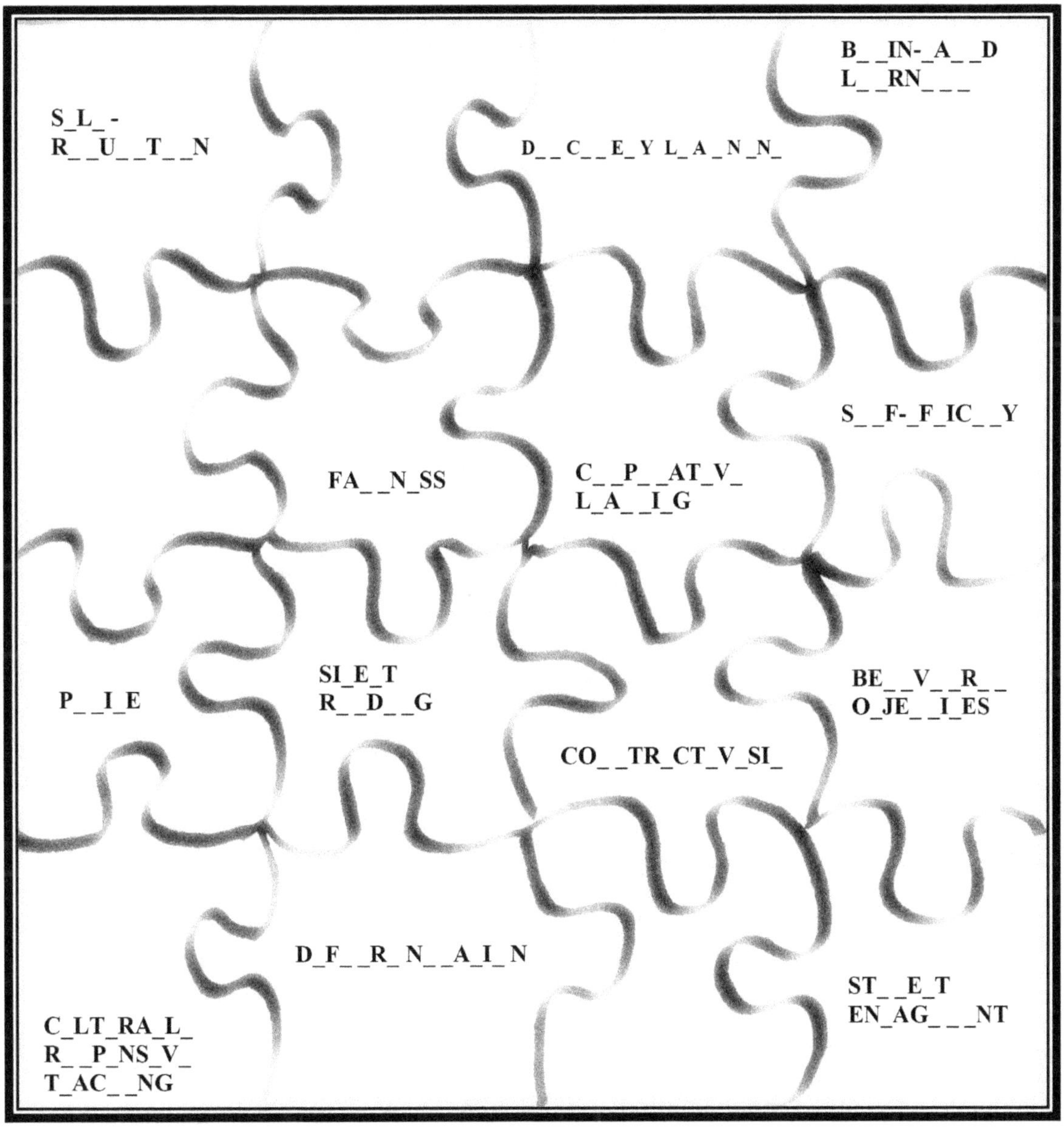

B_ _IN- _A_ _D
L_ _RN_ _ _

S_L_-
R_ _U_ _T_ _N

D_ _C_ _E_ Y L_A_ N_ N_

S_ _F- F_ IC_ _Y

FA_ _N_SS

C_ _P_ _AT_V_
L_A_ _I_G

P_ _I_E

SI_E_T
R_ _D_ _G

BE_ _V_ _R_ _
O_JE_ _ _I_ES

CO_ _TR_CT_V_SI_

D_F_ _R_N_ _A_I_N

ST_ _E_T
EN_AG_ _ _NT

C_LT_RA_L_
R_ _P_NS_V_
T_AC_ _NG

Answers for Exercise 5.1: Piecing Together Best Practices for Better Teaching

Self-Regulation   Discovery Learning
Brain-Based Learning   Fairness
Cooperative Learning   Self-Efficacy
Praise   Silent Reading
Constructivism   Behavioral Objectives
Differentiation   Culturally Responsive Teaching
Student Engagement

Exercise 5.2: Part I for Evidence-based Teaching Evaluations

Instructions: Add additional evidence for each solution to each problem in the blank spaces below.

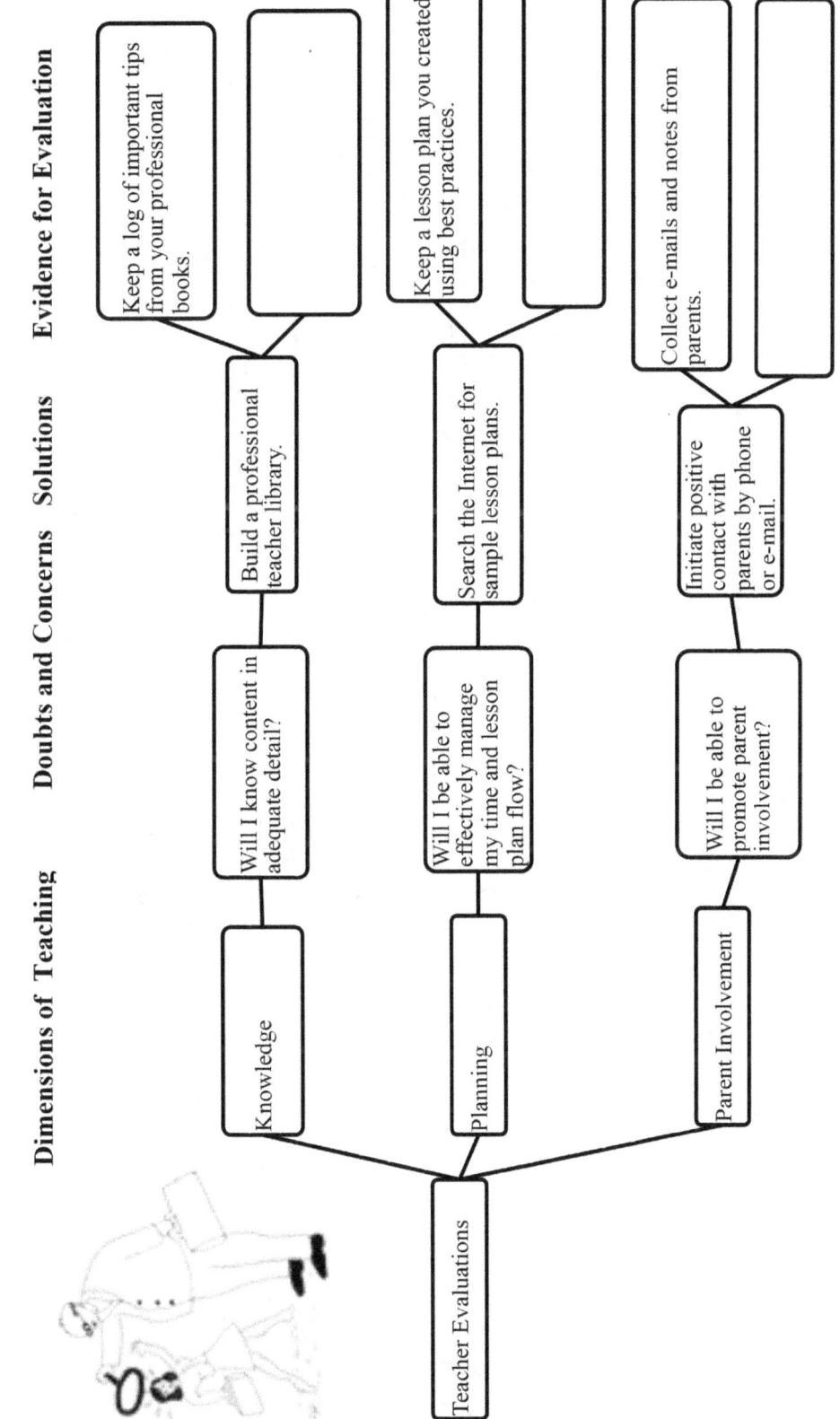

Exercise 5.2 Part II for Evidence-based Teaching Evaluations.

Instructions: Add additional evidence for each solution to each problem in the blank spaces below.

Dimensions of Teaching	Doubts and Concerns	Solutions	Evidence for Evaluation
Professional Development	Will I be weak in some areas of teaching?	Take advantage of district in-service training and workshops.	Ask for a certificate of participation for school in-service or workshops.
Quality and delivery of instruction	Will I be able to be creative considering I have to teach to the test.	Research best-teaching practices on the Internet.	Document research results on: teaching required content creatively.
Professionalism	Can I keep feelings of stress and frustration under control?	Have a repertoire of skills and alternatives to use as alternatives	Document how you used an alternative strategy to diffuse a situation to parents.
Assessment	Will I be able to be fair and unbiased?	Use rubrics for every lesson.	Keep copies of progress reports sent to parents.

Teacher Evaluations

Exercise 5.2: Part III for Evidence-based Teaching Evaluations

Instructions: Add additional evidence for each solution to each problem in the blank spaces below.

Dimensions of Teaching	Doubts and Concerns	Solutions	Evidence for Evaluation
Student Learning	Will I be able to make learning fun and interactive?	Seek student input on their likes, dislikes, preferences.	Keep an exemplary, fun student project as an artifact.
Classroom Management	Will I be able to deal with discipline problems?	Ask master teachers to tell how they handle discipline problems.	Document discipline problems, if any, for each child and how they were resolved.
Student Diversity	Will I be able to handle a multicultural classroom?	Learn something about the culture of each student in your class.	Respond to student entries about their culture in their journal and keep a sample.
Communication	Will I be able to help my students understand the material?	Ask a student volunteer to explain what you just taught.	Use a suggestion box to ask students what would help them to better understand the material.

All dimensions connect to: **Teacher Evaluations**

Exercise 5.3: Blueprint for Managing Risks Associated with Uncertainty

Instructions: List uncertainties or areas of risk that you are aware of in your teaching. Assess and analyze those uncertainties. List prevention strategies for avoiding risks. If risk is inevitable, list possible policies for assuming risk and managing uncertainty.

⊗ Ascertain uncertainties and risks inherent in your teaching.

1. Teaching content such as science lab
2.

⊗ Assess what or who is vulnerable to risk or threat?

1. Student safety, job security
2.

⊗ Analyze the magnitude of the risk or threat.

1. Student safety-moderate risk
2.
3.

⊗ Avoid risk with prevention.

1. Train students on the proper use of equipment and make them aware of safety rules.
2.
3.

⊗ Assume the risk, to try to minimize the effects through risk-sharing.

1. Monitor students for safety, and share the risk with parents by sending safety rules home for parents to review with children and sign the form as acknowledgment.
2.
3.

6

Managing the Brute Creations of Negative Emotions

Happy cats don't make good tigers. No more anger management classes for you.

The intoxication of anger, like that of the grape, shows us to others, but hides us from ourselves.

—Charles Caleb Colton

HARNESSING ANGER THROUGH ANGER MANAGEMENT

Incivility and anger in the classroom setting has increased exponentially over the years (Porterfield & Carnes, 2009). Anger-based conflict arises from negative interactions of teachers and students, teachers and parents, and teachers and colleagues. In today's high-tech world of violent television and video games, teachers and students are exposed to a constant electronic diet of anger and aggression. It is not surprising that these behaviors manifest in the classroom when teachers or students react to perceived conflicts or hurts. Teachers must take charge of managing their personal anger and the anger expression of their students.

There are two approaches to managing anger: conceptualizing anger and understanding the "why" of anger. Conceptualizing anger involves determining the scope of the anger problem. Namka (1997) proposes two strategies for managing anger. The first strategy is recognizing when anger is not a big deal, in other words, asking oneself, How important is this? Does it warrant extreme acting out, such as anger responses?

A second strategy is recognizing that people don't always get their way. Praise-and-ignore is a behavioral strategy used by many teachers to preserve order in the classroom. They praise good behavior and ignore unwanted behavior when appropriate, thereby minimizing their possible angry reaction to bad behavior. Even if teachers cannot ignore bad behavior, they need not have an angry reaction to it; they can choose to be calm and effective.

Using the second strategy requires a mature outlook of acceptance that teachers don't always get their way.

Some teachers prefer the quiet classroom with no student disturbances and where the teacher does most of the talking. This classroom format is no longer viable in the new age of student-centered learning and teaching. Unexpected outcomes are a constant in today's classrooms. The calm, effective teacher understands and accepts this fact of educational life and prepares for the unexpected rather than having an angry reaction to it. Teachers who have frequent anger responses to their students' behaviors run the risk of overreacting to student behavior and causing duress or harm to their students.

The key to unlocking teacher anger is seeking to understand the "why" of the anger. Teachers, like most people, react to perceived threats to the self. Some identified threats to the self are as follows:

- Feeling betrayed
- Being treated unfairly
- Feeling humiliated
- Being ignored or ostracized
- Being ridiculed
- Being cheated
- Being hurt
- Being disrespected

For many teachers, actual or perceived student disrespect is a major source of anger. Once teachers understand the "why" of their anger, they can start to develop healthy coping responses to perceived threats to their selves. Teachers cannot always control student behavior, but they can control how they react to it. They can begin by accepting that anger behavior is usually based on perceptions and how one feels and not necessarily on absolute truths. For example, simply because a student makes a derogatory remark about the teacher does not make it true.

Therefore, the calm teacher realizes it is not necessary to react emotionally to the comment and addresses inappropriate comments in a professional manner. Another response might be to listen intently to the student's concerns, avoiding patronizing and keeping an open mind, and then to address the problem and take appropriate action. In response to inappropriate behavior, teachers should be cautious and choose words carefully to avoid inflammatory language that might exacerbate the causal problem. Teachers can choose to respond professionally, preserving the dignity of themselves and their students.

Many effective teachers respond with understanding, integrity, mercy, and forgiveness, eliminating the need for anger. Sometimes it is necessary for teachers to help students and parents manage their anger to maintain a calm environment that is conducive to learning. Teachers should keep in mind that parents and students also want respect; it is prudent for the teacher to be respectful of everyone, including students. To encourage harmony, teachers may opt to include parents in strategic planning and decision making that affect their children's learning and well-being.

Porterfield and Carnes (2009) propose that parents and students want self-esteem, security, and justice; teacher behaviors should employ these constructs whenever interacting with parents and students. Positive teacher anger management behaviors can help students dismantle their mask of anger. They can help students diffuse their anger by teaching them positive strategies for protecting their self-esteem. They can establish teacher–student trust in small ways every day (Porterfield & Carnes, 2009), such as being polite to and respectful of each other.

Listening and allowing students to vent may be sufficient to help students diffuse their anger; teachers should teach their students to do the same with others. Healthy coping responses to anger will be beneficial to teachers, students, and the classroom environment.

FRUSTRATING FRUSTRATION WITH AWARENESS, AVOIDANCE, AND ACCEPTANCE

Frustration is a feeling of irritation or annoyance that accompanies a person's perception that one's goals or desires are thwarted or somehow hindered. Most teachers experience at least one frustrating classroom event at some point in their careers. Amsel and Roussel (1952) theorize that frustration is a motivational state resulting from nonreinforcement of responses that were previously reinforced.

An example might be a teacher who has been consistently reinforced for having good classroom control. One day, a student rebels, becomes disrespectful, and resists any of the teacher's attempts to discipline him. The state of the teacher experiences from this nonrewarding, nonreinforcing lack of control is frustration. When the disruptive student stops the behavior and order is restored to the classroom (reinforcing reward), frustration reduction may occur.

Considering that frustration may express as undesirable behavior, it is prudent to reduce or avoid it. Spector (1978) says that aggression is one of the behavioral effects of frustration. Some teachers resort to aberrant or inappropriate behavior when faced with frustrating student misbehavior. To manage frustration, one must be aware that they are feeling the sting of frustration. Awareness is an alert consciousness of an emotional reaction or an act of knowing. There are several ways that teachers can promote awareness. The following tips for preventing or dealing with frustration will help teachers acquire awareness and to use that awareness to minimize their frustration:

Awareness

- Teachers should note that the multidimensional, unpredictable nature of teaching dictates that many things may be beyond a teacher's control (Woolfolk, 2013).
- Teachers should know when their emotional stability is teetering on the brink and seek help from mentors or master teachers.
- Teachers should remind themselves often of the things that they happen to love about teaching.
- Teachers should exercise restraint, knowing that many frustrating events will eventually pass and that they may not have to act on them.
- Teachers should stay in touch with their feelings and know that they are powerless over controlling some students' negative or poor behavior but recognize that they have the power to control how they react to it.
- Teachers should choose not to react impulsively; rather, they should choose to calmly resolve issues and always be aware of students' feelings when grading their papers or commenting on their responses to questions.
- Teachers should be aware of students' body language that indicates frustration, such as facial expressions, posture, and gestures, to help them find the source of student frustration and deal with it appropriately.
- Teachers should stay cognizant of the features of great teaching, reflect on them, and celebrate them every day to avoid boredom, resentment, criticism, and fears.

- Teachers should become aware of their personal traits that inspire rebellion in their students, such as the following:

   Teaching mostly from the text
   Presenting content as boring, lengthy lectures without media
   Having an inability to answer questions correctly
   Having limited knowledge of the content being taught
   Having an attitude of superiority and condescension
   Not learning students' names or something about them
   Displaying a lack of caring or interest in students
   Displaying a lack of empathy for students, their issues, or their problems
   Being disorganized and unprepared for class
   Being unfair or biased in the grading or treatment of students

To find strategies for correcting their undesirable traits, teachers should stay abreast of advances, trends, and updates in the delivery of educational content and how such changes might enhance their teaching. They should be skillful in their use of electronic media and applications. Anticipating frustration may lead to avoidance of a task (Perry, Bussey, & Redman, 1977). The most effective escape from frustration is eluding it or preventing it from ever happening. The following tips are useful for avoiding frustration:

Avoidance

- Minimize assuming responsibility for extra work or tasks that do not benefit your career aspirations or your students' education.
- Be proactive and recruit parents as advocates who encourage their children to behave and cooperate and thereby avoid some problems in the classroom. If you share more positives than negatives about student performance with parents, they may be encouraged to become more involved and cooperative.
- Resist constant complaining and criticism to avoid fueling your negative feelings.
- Take an inventory of your activities inside and outside the classroom and subsequently determine which activities can be eliminated, minimized, or made more enjoyable to avoid being overwhelmed.
- Use rubrics that are self-explanatory, accurate, and efficient to minimize stress associated with grading papers.
- Recognize that you will never receive combat pay, so avoid combative situations and conflict as much as possible.
- Develop a professional friendship with parents before any problems arise by listening to them, welcoming them, and working together for the best interest of the students. This may help you avoid frustrating experiences with parents

in the future. Additionally, if a bad situation should occur with a student, the parents may be more receptive to helping resolve the problem.
- Heated confrontations with parents can be avoided by making every effort to diffuse the parents' anger before discussing any problems with difficult students.
- Avoid reactive frustration that results from your unsuccessful efforts to control or discipline students that can possibly erupt into undesirable outcomes, such as student mistreatment. Use prevention strategies and effective student engagement to frustrate potential discipline problems.
- Use technology whenever possible to decrease the workload, spark student interest, and thereby minimize frustration and stress.
- Identify ways to help stay calm and less reactive under pressure, such as thinking before speaking or taking a long pause to diffuse tension.
- Recognize that although you have a need for dignity and respect, that need should not outweigh student well-being. Avoid improper judgment calls in your emotional and behavioral responses to students' perceived disrespect or disruption and react only in ways that would be acceptable in a parent's presence. Accepting limitations on responses to student misbehavior is a powerful antidote for frustration because it replaces the sting of frustration and annoyance with a disposition of tolerance, peace, and understanding. The following tips for acceptance are beneficial in achieving this desired disposition.

Acceptance

- Frustrate the discontent that threatens the great teaching experience by nurturing an attitude of gratitude. Be thankful for the work opportunity and having the knowledge and ability to carry it out. Make a genuine effort to love your work, use positive affirmations, or create something to love about it.
- Seek first to understand the threat to the self behind students who are exhibiting unacceptable behavior; try not to react to it and help students resolve, understand, and accept their part in the problem.
- Admit when you can't resolve a situation in spite of efforts to address it and seek help to find a solution.
- Decide on an appropriate plan of action; pass it on to administration only if resolution is critical and it may happen again or ignore it and move on if it is a one-time occurrence that is not likely to happen again.
- Although teachers want to change the world of education and make a difference or have an impact, they must accept their limitations and make the best of hindrances that could get in the way of their making a difference, such as integrating creativity and innovation whenever possible.

- Teaching to the test is frustrating; accept that standardized testing is here to stay.
- Accept nonteaching duties that you detest by making them enjoyable, positive opportunities of engagement with students.
- Do your best to teach what is mandated, use best practices, address competencies, and accept that there are other variables that may affect outcomes. Relax when you know you've done your best; until then, don't stress. Get busy doing what needs to be done.
- Acknowledge that teaching has good and bad moments; celebrate the good moments that occur daily and that fuel a love of teaching.
- Acknowledge the stress inherent in the teaching job and find ways to lessen anxiety and boost serenity levels, such as through meditation, calming teas, yoga, exercise, and hobbies.
- Accept and work on what you can control and develop the wisdom to know when you can't so that you can accept uncontrollable circumstances and move on.

MULTIDIRECTIONAL SOURCES OF STRESS AND PRESSURE

Student Personal Problems and Issues

- Abuse
- Death
- Divorce
- Illness
- Poverty
- Neglect
- Homelessness
- Alcoholism
- Pregnancy
- Violence
- Anger
- Drug/alcohol abuse
- Sexual abuse

Special Needs

- Appropriate accommodations
- Individualized education plan

Nonteaching Duties

- Monitoring duties
- Committees
- Parent conferences
- Professional development

Teaching

- Grading assignments
- Discipline
- Administrative work
- Demonstrations
- Presentations
- Student records

Schoolwide

- Standardized testing
- Faculty meetings
- Curriculum competencies or standards

Teacher Roles

- Psychologist
- Child protective services
- Nurse
- Social worker
- Police

At the beginning of the school year, teachers are excited about teaching. After a few weeks, the honeymoon is over; stress and frustration become frequent visitors as demands, directives, needs, and student issues mount. Below are some teachers' possible responses to frustration:

- Screaming or yelling
- Pulling hair
- Snarling and threatening
- Swearing or cussing
- Making obscene body gestures

- Banging head on the board
- Putting head down and crying
- Putting head in hands
- Laughing hysterically
- Becoming sad and withdrawn
- Throwing hands up in the air
- Sitting and staring
- Throwing something
- Hitting or kicking something
- Mustering the resolve to do better
- Burning out
- Sulking or pouting
- Vowing to get even

LOSING THE EMOTIONAL BAGGAGE OF NEGATIVE EMOTIONS

Over the years, many people pick up and continue to carry unresolved issues of hypothetical emotional baggage that may negatively impact their future interactions with people. Some people carry a heavier load than others. Too much negative baggage invites dysfunction and lower quality of life. The problem with carrying around emotional baggage is that it tends to weigh one down and may consequently trip one up in future endeavors.

Some teachers may be abusing various substances, but many are just suffering from exposure to traumatic or disturbing events that occurred in childhood and that still have the power to generate emotion in adulthood (Orange, 2005). Emotional baggage has many tags, such as anger, rage, depression, anxiety, resentment, jealousy, and envy. Over the years, negative emotional events and feelings become important because the brain is wired to remember negative feelings or aversive events so that it can recognize and avoid them in the future.

Needless to say, the mental baggage of the brain can become overwhelming. Knowledge of the workings of the brain can help teachers discard unwanted baggage. They should begin by recognizing that the brain makes assumptions, associations, or interpretations that appear logical but that are not always accurate—much like the auto-correct feature on a computer. Most of the time, auto-correct may be useful, but its suggestions must be discarded when they are not accurate. Only the author can determine when assumed corrections to the document are correct or incorrect.

Likewise, teachers can try to determine if their brains are making erroneous assumptions and presenting them as truths that have been compromised by emotional baggage and make haste to discard those assumed truths. The content of emotional baggage may come from abuse as a child, unreasonable expectations from significant others, dysfunctional parenting, unhealthy adult relationships, and any other circumstance that will cause the teacher to view current situations through the tainted lens of past relationships, experiences, and abuses.

Such subconscious, distorted viewpoints inevitably will have a detrimental impact on a teacher's current work and interactions with her students and colleagues. Teachers' students and colleagues also can be instrumental in helping teachers discard their unwanted emotional baggage if their input is acknowledged or sought. If teachers encourage students to give honest feedback in class and in informal evaluations, they may gain some insight into their own behaviors, negative feelings, and reactions.

Teachers will benefit if they pay attention to their students' and colleagues' comments, criticisms, and complaints. The best way to lose emotional baggage is to fail to claim it. As soon as feelings are recognized as negative emotions, teachers could make an effort to lose them by making mental notes, such as "That's not my bag, and I'm not taking it with me." An example might be a teacher recognizing her feelings of jealousy of her colleagues who received a lot of praise and encouragement from the principal.

Such feelings of jealousy may be reminiscent of sibling rivalry in childhood where parents showed favoritism and better treatment to younger siblings. She could refuse to claim that "jealousy bag," wish her colleagues well, remind herself of something that she did that she was proud of, and make plans to improve her teaching where she perceives there might be a weakness.

She could also make efforts to resolve her sibling rivalry issues of the past. The negative outcomes and effects of emotional baggage are many: ineffective teaching, burnout, perfectionism, mistreatment of students, erosion of relationships with colleagues, low productivity, and poor performance evaluations, to name a few. Employing positive feelings of understanding, caring, praise, forgiveness, and encouragement of others is useful for rejecting unwanted baggage.

Sometimes professional help is needed to help troubled teachers unpack the many mental remnants of unresolved wrongs, humiliations, hurts, traumas, and negative experiences of the past. Self-help may be an option if the nature of the emotional baggage is not too severe or extensive. However, help in some form is critical to prevent manifestations of troubling, detrimental effects that carrying around emotional baggage can have on teachers' competence as educators.

REFERENCES

Amsel, A., & Roussel, J. (1952). Motivational properties of frustration: I. Effect on a running response of the addition of frustration to the motivational complex. *Journal of Experimental Psychology, 43*(5), 363.

Namka, L. (1997). Positive anger skills: Be a gentle, loving person even when you are mad. http://www.angriesout.com/grown3.htm

Orange, C. (2005). *44 smart strategies for avoiding classroom mistakes*. Thousand Oaks, CA: Corwin.

Perry, D. G., Bussey, K., & Redman, J. (1977). Reward-induced decreased play effects: Reattribution of motivation, competing responses, or avoiding frustration? *Child Development, 48*(4), 1369–1374.

Porterfield, K., & Carnes, M. (2009). Anger management. *School Administrator, 66*(7), 20–24.

Spector, P. E. (1978). Organizational frustration: A model and review of the literature. *Personnel Psychology, 31*(4), 815–829.

Woolfolk, A. E. (2013). *Educational psychology* (12th ed.). Boston: Pearson Education.

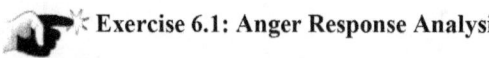 **Exercise 6.1: Anger Response Analysis**

Instructions: Circle the response that is most representative of your response to each scenario. Tally all 1's, 2's, 3's, and 4's; find the number that you circled the most and match that number with the number on the profile wheel that follows, to reveal your anger profile.

A coworker makes the faculty meeting go overtime by asking many questions on the same topic. 1. Groan out loud, saying "Again? Give me a break." 2. Slip out the door and go home. 3. Angrily whisper to others "what is her problem?" 4. Gently remind the convener of the policy of ending the meetings on time.
Students playing in the hall bump into you, making you spill hot coffee. 1. Call the students morons. 2. Say nothing, but think they are heathens. 3. Fume furiously and vow to give them trouble next time you see them. 4. Assertively call the students back, demand an apology and caution them about running in the halls because they could have caused a hot coffee burn.
A coworker takes credit for your work and gets a bonus. 1. Loudly confront the thief in front of others. 2. Decide never to speak to her again. 3. Plot to steal and claim some of her work. 4. Say, "I think you mistakenly turned in my report. I have evidence that I've been working on it for weeks. Would you like to tell the principal or should I do it?"
Students continue to laugh and laugh after you told them several times to be quiet. 1. Scream, "Shut up, I'm not going to tell you again" 2. Try to teach anyway. 3. Plan on giving everyone that's laughing a grade of "F". 4. Find out what's so funny and join in the laughter before asking the students to settle down.
An angry parent yells at you and calls you a poor teacher because her child is failing. 1. Say, "It's not my fault if your child is not smart." 2. Say, "Sorry I can't talk now, I have a meeting" 3. Plan to pay her back by giving her child a hard time. 4. Say, "Sorry you feel that way, but we both want what's best for your child. I suggest we work together to get your child's grades up."
The principal calls you out in a faculty meeting for your students having poor test scores. 1. Retort, "What do you expect when you consider what I have to work with?" 2. Excuse yourself and go to the restroom. 3. Think, "The principal better not make any mistakes. I'm going to be the first to call him on it." 4. Be sincere and tell the principal you are open for suggestions from him and the faculty.

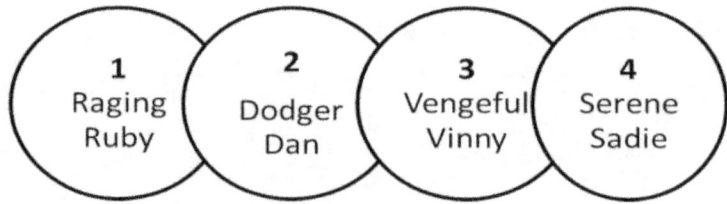

Exercise 6.2: Red Heat Rating

Instructions: For each of the frustration items that apply to you, circle the number of peppers that reflect your level of frustration and put the number of circled peppers in the box to the right.

Peppers	Item	
🌶🌶🌶🌶🌶	1. I am frustrated by my administration's lack of respect for teachers.	
🌶🌶🌶🌶🌶	2. I am frustrated when students don't do what I asked them to do.	
🌶🌶🌶🌶🌶	3. I am frustrated because I can't seem to get organized.	
🌶🌶🌶🌶🌶	4. I am frustrated when students don't do their homework.	
🌶🌶🌶🌶🌶	5. I am frustrated when my lessons fail.	
🌶🌶🌶🌶🌶	6. I am frustrated when my students are out of control.	
🌶🌶🌶🌶🌶	7. I am frustrated with parents who never come to parent competences.	
🌶🌶🌶🌶🌶	8. I am frustrated when I can't seem to get all of my work done for the day.	
🌶🌶🌶🌶🌶	9. I get frustrated when my students say "I don't understand" after I've just explained a topic.	
🌶🌶🌶🌶🌶	10. I get frustrated when I have to wait for students to answer questions.	
🌶🌶🌶🌶🌶	11. I am frustrated when I have to teach to the test.	
🌶🌶🌶🌶🌶	12. I feel frustrated when I hear about other teachers' accomplishments.	
🌶🌶🌶🌶🌶	13. I feel frustrated when I don't get the recognition I feel I deserve.	
🌶🌶🌶🌶🌶	14. I am frustrated when I don't have enough materials or supplies to do my job.	
🌶🌶🌶🌶🌶	15. I get frustrated when students continue to be rude to me and I can't stop.	
🌶🌶🌶🌶🌶	16. I am frustrated when administrators criticized my teaching and I don't think I can do better.	
🌶🌶🌶🌶🌶	17. I am frustrated when I send students to the principal's office and they send them back with no consequences.	
🌶🌶🌶🌶🌶	18. I am frustrated when disrespectful or disruptive students have a smirk on their faces.	
🌶🌶🌶🌶🌶	19. I feel frustrated when punishing students and they act as if my punishment doesn't bother them.	
🌶🌶🌶🌶🌶	20. I am frustrated when students seem to be laughing at me and I can't stop it.	
	Total	

RED HEAT INDEX

100-80 PEPPERS	🌶	ACUTE FRUSTRATION—At risk of harming students
79-60 PEPPERS	🌶	CHRONIC FRUSTRATION—At risk of burnout
59-40 PEPPERS	🌶	MODERATE FRUSTRATION—At risk of being overwhelmed
39-0 PEPPERS	🌶	MILD FRUSTRATION—Need more time quiet time to think

Exercise 6.3: Lose The Baggage of Negative Thinking and Reclaim Your Positive Thinking

Instructions: Read the list of possible negative messages and select 7 messages that resonate with you. Identify each by circling its number and writing the same number on one of the bags on the conveyor belt. Reclaim your positive thoughts by writing a positive thought on the claim ticket associated with the numbered bag. For example the bag with number 1 on it is associated with negative message number 1: 1. I will not try because I don't like the way failure feels. Repeat the process for each negative message you select. Don't forget to reclaim your positive thinking on the appropriate claim ticket.

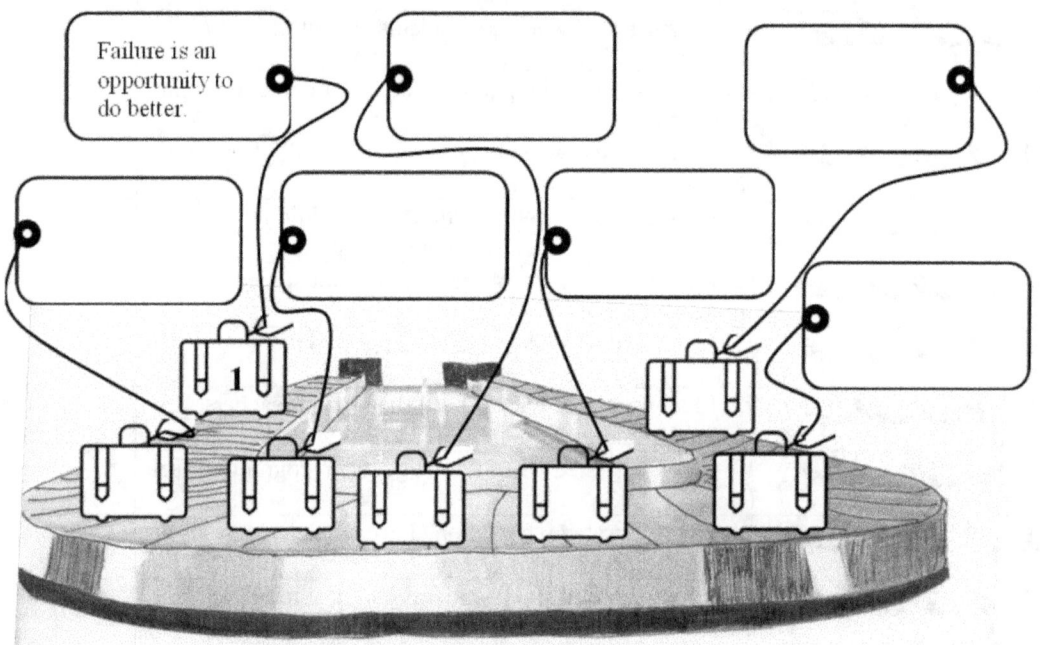

Negative Messages
1. I will not try because I don't like the way failure feels.
2. Other teachers are better at this than I am.
3. I have no instructions, so how can I do it?
4. I don't know where to begin.
5. I'm not very good at motivating students.
6. Teaching is difficult.
7. My lesson plans are never very good.
8. I'm afraid to ask for help; it will make me look weak.
9. Not everyone was meant to do well.
10. I'm uncertain when I have to choose; suppose I choose wrong?

Phase III

NEW CONNECTS: GENERATING NEW THINKING AND CONNECTING TO THE SUPER TEACHER WITHIN

7

Moving beyond Doubt to Enlightenment
Getting to Know the Professional You Better

I couldn't see for 20 years, and all it took was 20 seconds of cleaning my glasses for me to see the real world.

Personality is to a man what perfume is to a flower.

—Charles Schwab

DEVELOPING WINNING INTERPERSONAL SKILLS

When asked to provide some characteristics of good teachers, 42 graduate education students responded with about 100 characteristics collectively. About 35% of those characteristics appear to be intrapersonal skills, and about 65% appear to be interpersonal skills. Intrapersonal skills refer to behaviors, actions, relationships, and reactions within one person, whereas interpersonal skills are behaviors, actions, relationships, or reactions that involve two or more people. Gardner (1983) says that interpersonal skills are a type of intelligence.

Lowman (1984) states that creating intellectual excitement and establishing positive student rapport are good interpersonal skills that result in great teaching. Interpersonal skills are important in teaching because they address personality, character, ethics, and other behaviors that are heavily influenced by genetics and upbringing. Interpersonal skills may be influenced by family, society, and past experiences.

Interpersonal skills are influenced by the fear of the effect on relationships, friendships, and careers; possible exposure of one's weaknesses and vulnerabilities; and the personal costs involved if an interaction outcome is unacceptable or inappropriate (Bordone, 2000). Examples of situations that require good interpersonal skills are telling a parent about a child's poor behavior in class, saying no to an administrator who wants teachers to stay very late almost every night, and confronting a colleague who has spread some lies but is a friend worth keeping,

Telling students that their academic performance is poor in a manner that keeps their egos intact requires strong interpersonal skills. For teachers, developing interpersonal and intrapersonal skills will provide a wide range of appropriate, effective responses when addressing difficult, interactive situations. An analysis of the survey results revealed the following seven recurring themes of highly desired interpersonal skills in teachers.

Teachers Should Be Respectful

Treating students with respect was the number one interpersonal trait that students thought must be present in teachers. Teachers should respect students' ideas and suggestions and not embarrass them or call them out when they make a mistake. Students felt that public reprimands or negative remarks were inappropriate and ineffective; they thought that teachers should praise publicly and punish privately. Woolfolk (2013) says that soft, private reprimands are most effective, which also supports the surveyed students' views.

Teachers Should Have Expert Knowledge of Students

Understanding student development and having knowledge of students ranked second. Understanding what can be expected at each stage of development arms the teacher with potent knowledge of students and their behaviors, thoughts, and actions. Knowledge of student backgrounds, family situations, and any other adverse circumstances makes it possible for teachers to be empathic and more understanding if the student is experiencing academic difficulties. Respondents felt that good teachers should exchange personal bits of information early, in the beginning of the school year or class, and make an effort to understand each student individually.

Teachers Should Be Good Communicators

Clarity is the key to happiness for most students; the clearer the assignment and the instructions, the better. According to the survey, students felt that teachers should use whatever materials or media are available and relevant to help students understand and relate to the material. Comprehension is improved when the teacher provides numerous anecdotes and examples. Good teachers should be great presenters, speakers, and listeners who are also entertaining and interesting.

Teachers Should Be Willing to Help Students

Students want an approachable human being who is always available and willing to help. They believe they should not be afraid to ask the teacher for help. Helping students and the warmly gratifying results of making a difference are the types of psychic income that make teaching worthwhile in spite of perceived salary limitations. Students want teachers to be willing to go the extra mile necessary to help them. They want teachers to look for students who need help, meeting students halfway down the path of needing help to make help seeking easier—a highly desirable self-regulatory behavior.

Teachers Should Be Encouraging, Motivating, and Inspiring

The survey results indicated that students want to be encouraged to be better. They want teachers who try to move students to action and help them realize their potential. Good teachers are an inspiration to their students; every day, they communicate to students that they believe in them. When assigning challenging material, good teachers communicate their confidence in their students' ability to successfully meet the challenge.

Teachers Should Affirm Diversity

Culturally responsive teaching (Gay, 2010) is a venue used by good teachers to address diversity issues. Students want teachers to appreciate each individual's uniqueness, to embrace individual differences, and to be responsive to any needs that may arise as a result of diversity. For example, teachers should pay attention to the social needs of special needs children and help them make friends, make it possible to go to prom, and so on.

Teachers Should Love to Teach

The enthusiasm and energy that exude from a teacher who loves her work and is passionate about teaching are contagious. Good teachers relate well to students, make learning fun, are never condescending, are open to suggestions, and see criticism as an opportunity to do better. Most of all, a teacher who loves to teach generally loves students; such teachers are caring, compassionate, and not afraid to show those feelings to their students every day.

Minimizing stress is a first step in improving interpersonal skills; a calm approach facilitates appropriate interaction with others (Escobar, 2007). There is strength in having effective interpersonal skills. When a teacher has strong interpersonal skills, discipline problems are minimized, stress is diminished, and job satisfaction and successful teaching outcomes are likely to increase.

DEVELOPING A STAR TEACHER PERSONA

Current research proposes that humans are made of stardust. Most elements on Earth, including humans, are made up of remnants of a supernova explosion that scattered various elements throughout the universe. Stars get their light from the energy that forms as a result of nuclear fusion reactions in their core. Some of the elements created from supernova remnants that combined with other elements as they moved through the universe make up the human body. Scientists believe that humans are 93% stardust (American Physical Society, 2015).

A lumen is a measurement of the brightness of light output. The more energy expended, the brighter the star. "Intelli-lumens" from human stars might be a measure of the level of knowledge, energy, creativity, and passion that one puts into a task that determines the brightness of the enlightenment outcome of that task and the resulting perception of that person as a performer. People who put a lot of energy, passion, knowledge, creativity, and so on into their work tend to shine brighter than others who extend much less energy and lack the requisite skills to shine.

Teachers, like other humans, are made up of stardust, and, like everyone else, they have the capacity to build a bright-star teaching persona in the classroom. As masters of their fate, they can determine how bright their stars shine by the energy they are willing to expend in all aspects of their teaching. The actions, interactions, and reactions that are at the core of their teaching are highly tumultuous, much like the microversions of nuclear fusion explosions that are continuously occurring in the core of stars all over the galaxy.

Constructing a star teaching persona necessitates maximizing important strength assets, such as skills, abilities, beliefs, talents, expertise, habits, cognitions, emotions, and behaviors. Teachers can heighten current skill levels by refining relevant cognitions and behaviors that will increase their efficiency and effectiveness; star teachers readily seek new skills that will enhance their teaching personas. Teachers who are endowed with talents will always seek to make maximum use of all their talents. Star teachers believe that they will succeed in whatever task they take on and that they will be resourceful enough to find a solution if they encounter problems.

REFERENCES

American Physical Society. (2015). How much of the human body is made up of stardust? http://www.physicscentral.com/explore/poster-stardust.cfm

Bordone, R. C. (2000). Teaching interpersonal skills for negotiation and for life. *Negotiation Journal, 16*, 377–385.

Escobar, J. (2007). Interpersonal skills. *Aircraft Maintenance Technology, 18*, 42–47.

Gardner, H. (1983). *Frames of mind: The theory of multiple intelligences.* New York: Basic Books.

Gay, G. (2010). *Culturally responsive teaching: Theory, research, and practice.* New York: Teachers College Press.

Lowman, J. (1984). *Mastering college teaching: Dramatic and interpersonal skills.* Paper presented at the National Institute on Teaching of Psychology to Undergraduates, Clearwater Beach, FL.

Woolfolk, A. E. (2013). *Educational psychology* (12th ed.). Boston: Pearson Education.

 **Exercise 7.1: Developing Interpersonal and Intrapersonal Skills**

Instructions: Look at the 100 winning interpersonal and intrapersonal skills of an effective teacher below and check the box for all that apply to you. Count the number of boxes checked to assess your interpersonal/intrapersonal skills level. Mark your score on the bell scale. If you fall into the skills training needed level, use the unchecked boxes as a guide for skills that you should work on to have better interpersonal/intrapersonal skills.

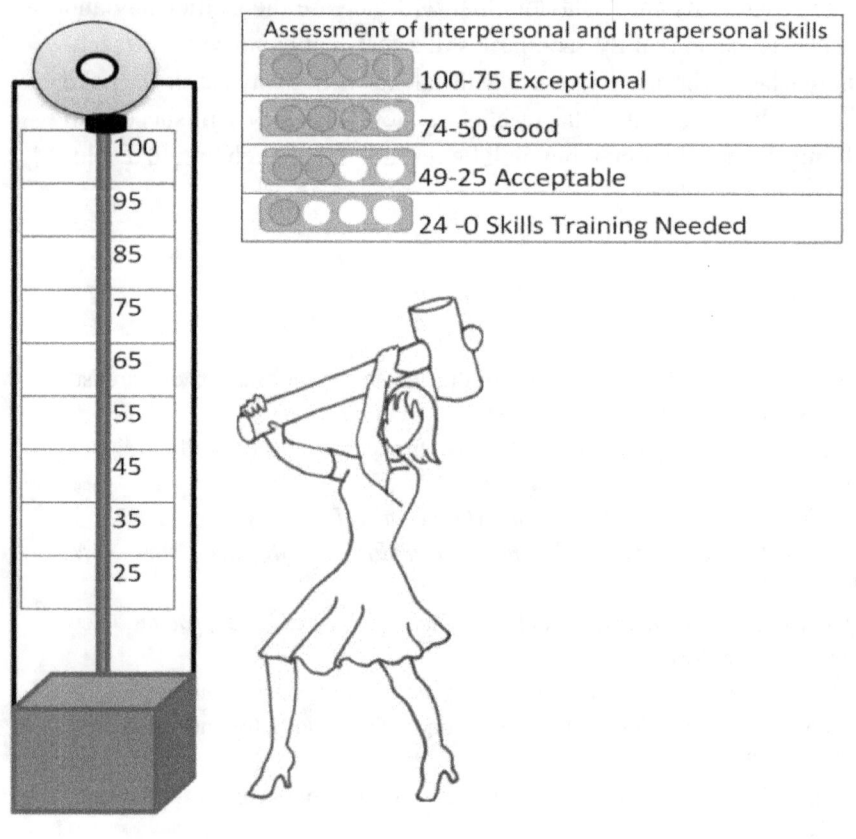

7.1 Continued: 100 Qualities of Effective Teachers

- ☐ awesome
- ☐ a role model
- ☐ accepts new challenges
- ☐ active
- ☐ affirms diversity
- ☐ alert
- ☐ has control of classroom
- ☐ approachable
- ☐ attentive
- ☐ authentic
- ☐ authoritative
- ☐ believes in students
- ☐ can admit mistakes
- ☐ can handle unexpected situations
- ☐ caring
- ☐ challenges their students
- ☐ checks for understanding frequently
- ☐ communicates well with parents
- ☐ compassionate
- ☐ continually seeks a better way to teach
- ☐ courteous
- ☐ creative
- ☐ culturally sensitive
- ☐ dedicated
- ☐ empathic
- ☐ empowering
- ☐ encourages critical thinking
- ☐ encourages students to ask questions
- ☐ encourages students to do better
- ☐ energetic
- ☐ enjoys teaching
- ☐ entertaining
- ☐ expressive
- ☐ exciting
- ☐ firm but kind
- ☐ flexible
- ☐ focused
- ☐ friendly
- ☐ fun
- ☐ gives best efforts in teaching
- ☐ good disciplinarian
- ☐ good interpersonal skills
- ☐ good listener
- ☐ good speaker
- ☐ good teaching strategies
- ☐ great communicator
- ☐ hard-working
- ☐ helps students realize their potential
- ☐ honest
- ☐ humor-loving
- ☐ innovative
- ☐ inspiring
- ☐ interacts with students individually
- ☐ interesting
- ☐ is fair
- ☐ keeps class engaged
- ☐ knowledge of students
- ☐ knowledge of teaching settings
- ☐ knowledge of subject matter
- ☐ leads by example
- ☐ lifelong learner
- ☐ likable
- ☐ loves to teach
- ☐ loving
- ☐ motivated
- ☐ nice
- ☐ nonbiased
- ☐ not boring
- ☐ not easily offended
- ☐ observing
- ☐ on task
- ☐ open to new ideas
- ☐ open-minded
- ☐ organized
- ☐ outgoing
- ☐ passionate
- ☐ patient
- ☐ personable
- ☐ positive
- ☐ praising
- ☐ presents information in several ways
- ☐ professional
- ☐ relates real world experiences to subjects
- ☐ relates well to students
- ☐ respectful
- ☐ respectful of students with special needs
- ☐ responsible
- ☐ responsive
- ☐ sense of humor
- ☐ sets goals
- ☐ skillful
- ☐ speaks clearly
- ☐ talented
- ☐ task-oriented
- ☐ understanding
- ☐ uses differentiation for a variety of learners
- ☐ uses research to teach effectively
- ☐ uses technology effectively
- ☐ well-prepared
- ☐ willing to help

Exercise 7.2: Assessing Your Star Teacher Persona

Instructions: Circle the rating that best describes where you think you rate for each persona characteristic in the table below. Sum your circled responses to get a subtotal for your negative responses and a subtotal of your positive responses. Add the subtotals to determine your overall Star Teacher Persona score and record it in the box. If your score is not what you want it to be, note the characteristics where you gave yourself a low rating and work to improve in that area.

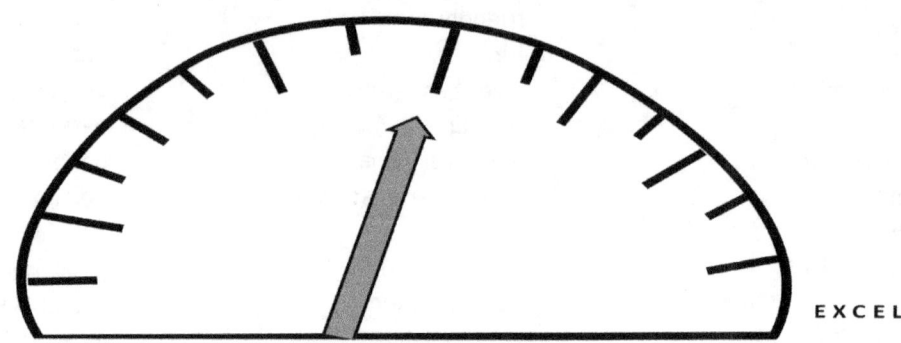

Persona-Meter

INEPT — EXCELLENT

Ratings			Persona Characteristics	Ratings		
-1	-2	-3	Personable	+1	+2	+3
-1	-2	-3	Rapport with Students	+1	+2	+3
-1	-2	-3	Pleasing Professional Appearance	+1	+2	+3
-1	-2	-3	Stage Presence	+1	+2	+3
-1	-2	-3	Voice Clear and Pleasing	+1	+2	+3
-1	-2	-3	Knowledge of Content	+1	+2	+3
-1	-2	-3	Ability to Motivate Students	+1	+2	+3
-1	-2	-3	Interesting Lessons	+1	+2	+3
-1	-2	-3	Work Well With Colleagues	+1	+2	+3
-1	-2	-3	Use A Variety of Media for Teaching	+1	+2	+3
-1	-2	-3	Courteous and Helpful	+1	+2	+3
-1	-2	-3	Completes Tasks in a Timely Fashion	+1	+2	+3
-1	-2	-3	Genuinely Cares About Students	+1	+2	+3
-1	-2	-3	High Enthusiasm is Apparent	+1	+2	+3
-1	-2	-3	Passionate About Teaching	+1	+2	+3
-1	-2	-3	Fair to All Students	+1	+2	+3
-1	-2	-3	Makes Teaching Fun	+1	+2	+3
-1	-2	-3	Talented In Many Areas	+1	+2	+3
-1	-2	-3	Uses Numerous Teaching Strategies	+1	+2	+3
-1	-2	-3	Cool Under Fire	+1	+2	+3
-1	-2	-3	Always Prompt	+1	+2	+3
Subtotal (-) =				Subtotal (+) =		
			Total Star Teacher Persona Score			

8

Creating Exceptional Educational Environments for Maximum Learning

I think I am finally getting all of my arms around this student engagement idea.

There are two ways of being creative. One can sing and dance. Or one can create an environment in which singers and dancers flourish.

—Warren Bennis

MASTERING THE ART OF STUDENT ENGAGEMENT: YOU CAN DO IT

Student engagement may be defined as the degree of interest, attentiveness, responsiveness, and commitment a student demonstrates when participating in educational activities and instruction. Engagement is measured on a continuum from minimum to maximum; minimum may be polite attention, slight interest, or low motivation whereas in maximum engagement, there is strong attention where the student is very engrossed in the task. Engaged students also display high interest, they want to know more, they ask questions, they persist when faced with difficulties and obstacles, and they are motivated to go beyond what is required.

The learning strategy is to move toward maximum engagement whenever possible. Group work in an active learning environment, such as collaboration cooperative project learning where students are free to interact with each other, free to secure the resources they deem necessary, seek solutions through trial and error tends to encourage higher levels of engagement. These students are inspired and energized by their successes. According to Klem and Connell (2004), higher levels of student engagement are linked to higher levels of student academic performance and achievement.

The military has rules of engagement that explain how to approach a situation. Likewise, teachers would do well to have rules of student engagement to move toward maximum engagement, such as the following:

Rule 1: Make maximum use of allotted time

- Provide small slots of time to teach study strategies.
- Overplan or have students present a strategy for using small amounts of time.
- Present brain-based activities, such as lateral thinking puzzles.
- Present student-created questions on the content taught that day.
- Present new words from the course content.
- Discuss motivational quotes.

Rule 2: Include real-world materials and events for study when appropriate

- Present current issues and take time to reflect on and discuss them.
- Assign critical reading of everyday items, such as food labels, newspapers, medicine warning sheets, loan application, credit card disclosures, and so on.
- Use current technology to stimulate interest.

Rule 3: Promote unrestricted inquiry

- Generate a list of questions for which they would like to have answers.
- Use the Internet to decide where they might find information.

- Send a letter by e-mail, mail, or text messaging to an appropriate contact and see if they get a response (that would include government agencies).
- Evaluate their responses to see whether they found the right answer to their question or whether should they try to contact another source.
- Contact at least three sources and compare the responses received for clarity and usefulness.
- Discuss their experiences with their group.

Rule 4: Encourage students to freely share their ideas with others

- Use strategies such as good graffiti (put sticky notes on the wall and give students colored markers; students write important ideas or concepts from what they are studying in different-colored markers on the sticky notes).
- Have students act as consultants for each other's projects.
- Have students exchange ideas in an online discussion forum.
- Have students work together in groups to solve problems.

Rule 5: Have numerous tactical learning experiences that deliver learning

- Game-based learning
- Brain-based learning
- Cooperative learning
- Collaborative learning
- Authentic learning
- Experiential learning
- Inquiry learning
- Tangential learning

Rule 6: Help students develop a positive attitude about school and learning

- Foster knowledge and understanding of the value of education.
- Urge students to embrace the long-term gratification and benefits of education.
- Explain how an education makes life better all-around and more financially profitable.
- Encourage risk taking where there are no stupid questions and the class is a laboratory where exploring answers is welcomed.
- Provide opportunities for students to succeed.
- Teach them the joys of self-satisfaction.
- Encourage social or peer interactions.
- Teach them to welcome a challenge using self-satisfaction as a reward.

Rule 7: Model personal investment, enthusiasm, and commitment to the task at hand

- Use techniques that foster a love of learning.
- Freely show excitement and enthusiasm about the learning task.
- Teach them to work without external reward and to be self-motivated.

Rule 8: Encourage students to make an accurate assessment of their self-knowledge and metacognition—knowing what they know, what they need to know, and why they need to know it before beginning a task

- Provide authentic assessment opportunities.
- Provide an opportunity to self-assess.
- Provide a variety assessments, such as group projects and activities, self-tests, portfolios, and peer assessments, to accommodate student understandings in a variety of contexts.

Rule 9: Employ a variety of cognitive strategies

- Consensus seeking
- Problem solving
- Persuasion
- Divergent thinking
- Critical thinking
- Challenging the status quo
- Providing evidence

Rule 10: Ensure that students have appropriate resources and fully functioning tools at their disposal

- Provide materials such as books, microscopes, computers, scientific equipment, and so on.
- Take students to the source of needed materials, such as archived photos, published narratives, museum artifacts, and so on, to generate authenticity and promote engagement.

Constructivism (Woolfolk, 2013) is an appropriate learning theory for maximizing student engagement. An example might be encouraging divergent thinking to promote student engagement through tangential learning. Tangential learning occurs when teachers allow or encourage students to explore tangents and see where they might lead them or find out more about their interests. This type of learning should be within a context that students enjoy (Brown, Rivera, Li, Wu, & Nguyen, 2013). The teacher is a facilitator, so make sure the tangents are relevant and not random and totally unrelated.

Teachers guide by recognizing a point of high interest as the students are working and discussing and inviting other students to explore the tangents. If students have questions, finding the answers by exploring their questions or topics that emerge from research can also take students into tangential directions. The following sequence of learning events in a lesson on types of transportation, in an enjoyable context of playing with cars, exemplifies tangential learning:

Student: *There are lots of types of transportation, but cars are the best.*

Guiding question: *Do you have any cars?*

Student: *Yes, I have lots of model cars in my collection.*

Guiding question: *Can you bring some of those to class tomorrow?*

Student: *Really? Sure, I can bring some cars tomorrow.*

[The next day]:

Student: *I brought some cars; you want to help me count them?*

Guiding question: *Wow! You've counted 82 cars. Do you know how many of them are red? Are there more red cars than the others?*

Student: *I don't know. I have to put the colors together to see how many are in each color.*

Guiding question: *Nice job. Do you think you can represent these colors on graph paper?*

Student: *Yes, if I may have some graph paper and markers. I also can use PowerPoint to make the graph.*

Guiding question: *Do you know the model of each one of your cars?*

Student: *I know some of them, but I could look them up on the Internet.*

Guiding question: *Great, you can also graph the models; perhaps you can create a pie chart in PowerPoint.*

Student: *I probably have more Chevys than any other cars. They are very popular.*

Guiding question: *How do you think car companies compete to make you buy their product instead of someone else's?*

Student: *They use advertising.*

Guiding question: *Can you create an ad and compare your ad to one of their ads when you have finished to see if your ad is as powerful as their ad?*

Student: *Of course, I just need some paper and pencil, and I'll create a great ad. I can find a sample of their ads on their website.*

Guiding question: *This is a great ad. Do you think you can write a paragraph or two on the ads and discuss how they are different or similar and which one is the most persuasive? Find a buddy in the class who likes cars and look up your favorite cars.*

Student: *That was a great project; we learned a lot about cars and dealerships. I called some dealerships to find the prices and the features that are available on my favorite cars. [This extra effort is a great example of tangential learning.] I also made a table to compare prices at various dealerships to see which one I would buy. I think Hondas were the best cars.*

Guiding questions: *Well, as a final activity, would you like to write about your experiences with the dealership in your journals?*

Student: *Sure, I think I have a lot to say.*

This tangential learning experience is just one way to engage students. However, it minimizes resistance to requests for learning activities that may be perceived as boring. In the tangential sequence presented previously, the student created graphs, categorized data, created ads, conducted research, and engaged in collaborative learning and journaling, all within the context of playing with his cars, an enjoyable activity. The transition to each activity was tangential and smooth because it was based on the student's interest, was student-centered and constructivist in approach, and moved toward maximum engagement.

MAKE YOURS A LIVING, BREATHING CLASSROOM

A field that has been seeded will fail to produce viable plants if growing essentials are not provided. Without water and nutrients, the poor soil becomes a parched, cracked growing medium that impedes plants' growth. Without sunlight and adequate air circulation, plants will wither, yellow, and drop their leaves or shrivel up and languish on dry vines. Students are much like plants in that they need a rich growing medium, nutrients, and an appropriate climate: a fertile environment that encourages innovation and intellectual risks, adequate cutting and pruning of anything that will constrict growth, and light for enlightenment and clarity.

In short, students would thrive in a greenhouse-like classroom that provided everything students need to grow. The greenhouse effect can change a dry, parched classroom into a living, breathing entity that pulsates with activity, creativity, and innovation. Such a classroom will oscillate with waves of light-drenched ideas, sway with rhythmic routines and practices, and break through mediocrity with creative activity and productivity. Such a classroom is not static; it is dynamic, giving the illusion of collective breathing in and out with the germination of stimulating activities and discoveries.

The following is a blueprint for making your classroom a living, breathing greenhouse:

1. Prepare a rich growing medium where students can grow in confidence. DeFrondeville (2009) recommends cultivating an environment that is psychologically safe for all students to learn and grow, considering that some risk taking is necessary; teachers must create an emotionally and intellectually safe classroom. Like preparing soil, loosen antiquated rules, restrictions, and beliefs to make the environment more student-centered. The physical work space should be colorful, adequate, and accommodating for individual and small-group work. Students should have plenty of mental and physical breathing room.
2. Temperature and climate should be ideal to foster good teacher–student relationships through mutual respect and improved rapport. In an ideal climate, students are cordial, caring, and respectful of each other; they feel that they will be treated and disciplined with dignity, even in conflict situations. Like the greenhouse climate, teachers are warm, exhibiting a high level of caring and sensitivity to students' needs.
3. Fertilizer for plants is the equivalent of motivation for students. In an enriched environment, students are willing to take intellectual risks, such as asking questions and exploring new approaches. They feel that their ideas are valued.
4. Openness and clarity simulate the airiness of a greenhouse. This is accomplished by presenting clear goals and minimal to no uncertainty. Class routines and procedures are clearly communicated. Establishing clear goals eliminates uncertainty in communicating assignments and expectations. These goals can be individual or group goals that are communicated effectively. Open communications are critical for clearing the air in the classroom and resolving conflict.
5. Tending the plants, pruning, and cutting are important greenhouse activities. In the greenhouse classroom, it is imperative to cut out practices that incite conflict and encourage teacher frustration. Teachers are mindful of situations and transitions that can result in classroom disruptions and respond with sensitivity. There is minimal conflict and a high level of caring.
6. Opportunities for teachers to "feed" and nurture their students abound in a greenhouse model. Play is an important element of an effective learning environment for teachers and students; play feeds the spirit and the soul and fills the air with laughter, the equivalent of "plant talk." Lundin, Paul, and

Christensen (2000) say that morale, energy levels, productivity, and creativity are boosted through play. Teachers have high expectations for student achievement and performance; they will make special efforts to develop the marginal performer. There are high standards of excellence; both teachers and students want high-quality work.

7. The greenhouse is all about light. Plants respond to light, and so will the students in the greenhouse classroom. This classroom will feature as much natural light as possible and be augmented, if necessary, with artificial light. Light is enlightening; it helps students and teachers see work as important and rewarding. Teachers and students see technology as an integral, necessary part of learning. Teachers clearly see the need for culturally sensitive materials (Gay, 2010) and respond appropriately. Teachers make sure to showcase students in their best light.

REFERENCES

Brown, T., Rivera, C., Li, H., Wu, A., & Nguyen, A. (2013). Development of tangential learning in video games. http://www.seas.upenn.edu/~cse400/CSE400_2013_2014/reports/07_report.pdf

deFrondeville, T. (2009). Ten steps to better student engagement: Project learning teaching strategies can also improve your everyday classroom experience. *Edutopia.* http://www.Edutopia.org/project-learning-teaching-strategies

Gay, G. (2010). *Culturally responsive teaching: Theory, research, and practice.* New York: Teachers College Press.

Klem, A. M., & Connell, J. P. (2004). *Linking teacher support to student engagement and achievement.* Paper presented at the 10th biennial meeting of the Society for Research on Adolescence, Baltimore.

Lundin, S. C., Paul, H., & Christensen, J. (2000). *Fish.* New York: Hyperion.

Woolfolk, A. E. (2013). *Educational psychology* (12th ed.). Boston: Pearson Education.

 **Exercise 8.1: Create a Tangential Learning Sequence Script**

Instructions: Develop a tangential learning experience using your choice of rules of engaging the student. Use the following template to write your script. Your questions and activities should be guided by anticipated student responses.

Topic to initiate discussion:

Student: _____.

Guiding question: _____?

Student: _____.

Guiding question: _____?

Student: _____.

Guiding question: _____?

Student: _____.

Guiding question: _____?

Student: _____.

Guiding question: _____?

Student: _____.

Guiding question: _____?

Student: _____.

Guiding question: _____?

Exercise 8.2: Create a Greenhouse Classroom

Instructions: Using the blueprint presented above, give examples of how you will make your classroom a living, breathing greenhouse for students. An example is provided for "nutrients."

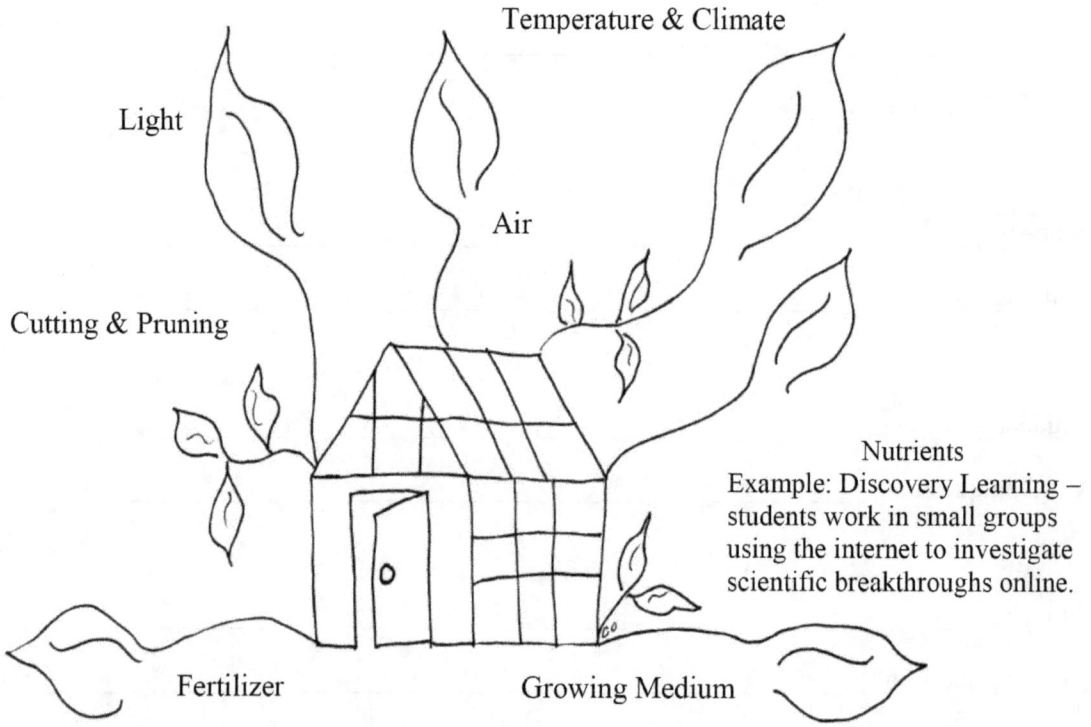

9

Exploring the Potency of Empowerment

Your new glasses make you look like super worm.

Believe in yourself and there will come a day when others will have no choice but to believe with you.

—Cynthia Kersey

TASTING THE SWEET FRUITS OF SELF-EMPOWERMENT: EMPOWER YOURSELF AND YOUR STUDENTS

To empower their students, teachers need to empower themselves first. Wilson (1993) proposes that teachers should develop a sense of personal power to create an empowered climate in their classrooms. No one can depend on others to empower them: the most dependable and effective source of empowerment is self-empowerment.

People who are self-empowered have an internal locus of control, meaning that they feel that their power originates from within and that they are in control of their lives (deCharms, 1977; Rotter, 1975). The classroom may become a source of conflict as teachers and students strive to be in control of their lives or to be what deCharms (1977) refers to as being an origin rather than a pawn who perceives that she is under another's control or at the mercy of external forces.

To avoid such power struggles, conflicts, and personal controversies in classrooms, teachers should strive to perceive themselves as origins and encourage their students to see themselves as having some control over their lives by creating a climate of shared power where children are active participants in the planning and activities of the class (Smith, 2004). Self-empowered people embrace the premise that the best source of authority comes from within and that their thoughts, beliefs, and feelings are worthwhile. Teachers possess talents, competencies, skills, and abilities that are just waiting to be released. However, teachers are the only ones who have the power and the authority to release their powers within. They must muster the courage to act and release their power.

Exotic Thai fruits are a great analogy for releasing the powers within. The power of exotic Thai fruits lies in the desired sweetness and textures inside the fruits' casings. Fruits such as durian, snake fruit, rambutan, jackfruit, and mangosteen all have strong casings that can range from easy to very hard to open. The mangosteen needs a firm squeeze to crack open the casing and release a sweet, delicious, white fruit that is in segments. This is analogous to a person building the confidence and determination to burst through the hard, spiky or sharp, spiny casings of self-doubt to release the sweet powers and traits of tenacity, resourcefulness, nonconformity, and multiple talents. The many segments of the mangosteen can be likened to the multiple intelligences in a person proposed by Gardner (1983).

The rambutan can be broken open with the fingers to release the fruit within. Nibbling the fruit is the best way to get it off the large center stone. Snake fruit has sharp spines that require a technique of pinching the tip of the fruit and peeling down to avoid the painful spines. Releasing the snake fruit and avoiding spines may be analogous to teaching ingenuity that is often used to avoid sticky situations.

Releasing the fruits of these exotic fruits becomes a collective metaphor for putting a mental squeeze on the brain to crack open the fruits of the mind, opening the person up to many possibilities, such as savoring the sweet fruits of inspiration, innovation, or revelation. Spiny, spiky, sharp casings may be a metaphor for self-doubt. Releasing the fruit of the rambutan is analogous to teacher resourcefulness, releasing the jackfruit may be analogous to teaching nonconformity, and releasing the durian may be analogous to teacher tenacity.

There are a number of ways teachers can empower themselves and encourage their students to do the same. Below are 11 tips for self-empowerment:

1. Revel in the knowledge that no one can make you do anything that you truly don't want to do. Know that there are consequences and have the willingness to accept them, good and bad, as the price of doing what you want. This action is tempered by prudence, good judgment, and wise choices.
2. Be proactive and take action; don't wait for directions from others.
3. Don't fear the expectations of others; know that you will meet them to the best of your ability and allow yourself to fail with dignity if you cannot meet expectations.
4. Find something that you do well and do it.
5. Take pride in your accomplishments—celebrate them.
6. Value and respect your thoughts and feelings.
7. Do not be deterred by criticism.
8. Start doing things for yourself that you used to rely on others to do for you.
9. Savor the praise you get from others. It will give you an idea of what others think of you, and, chances are, they may see you in a more favorable light than you see yourself. Be willing to try new or unfamiliar things.
10. Find enjoyment and inspiration being around strong, accomplished people rather than feeling intimidated by them.
11. Don't always opt for the easy, soft way; sometimes the seemingly impossible yields the best rewards.

After using the 11 tips, your empowered classroom would look like a self-empowered teacher is at the helm, one who uses ingenuity, innovation, resourcefulness, and other traits to share the sweet fruits of empowerment with her students.

PUTTING A CAN-DO MASK ON YOUR DOUBT AND HELPING YOUR STUDENTS PUT ONE ON THEIRS

The tangible mask is verifiable and real, whereas imaginary masks are decorative and not verifiable. Sometimes they are difficult or almost impossible to detect. An imaginary mask is usually a false persona developed by a person to conceal true feelings or truths. This mask is designed to look like truth. It often covers for socially unacceptable emotions, such as jealousy, envy, anger, resentment, and so on. Although some teachers may wear such masks at times to cover their feelings and truths, it is the mask that covers their doubts that may influence their effectiveness as a teacher. A mask of doubt may also affect students who tend to mimic some of their teachers' behaviors.

Teachers, like other people, wear masks for a variety of reasons; most of these reasons respond to a real or perceived inadequacy, such as a mask of bragging about their college grades because they feel that their teaching credentials are inadequate for the course they are assigned to teach. Some may act as if they care for a particular ethnic group when they don't, but they don't want to be judged unfavorably by others. There are numerous reasons why people wear masks:

- To appear confident when they are not
- To avoid appearances of being socially or politically incorrect
- To hide tears
- To feel safe psychologically
- To please others and gain love or approval
- To cope with difficulty
- To fool others or to be deceptive

Maslow's (1968) hierarchy of needs explains some of the needs behind the masks, such as safety, self-esteem, and love needs.

The teacher's effectiveness is diminished by the negatives associated with masking. For teachers, wearing a mask makes it difficult to have meaningful relationships with colleagues, parents, and students. Teachers who engage in masking often lose touch with the real, authentic person behind the mask, blurring the lines between farce and reality. An unfortunate by-product of teacher-masking behavior is the effect it could have on the children in their charge. Students are perceptive: they might see the dissonance inherent in teachers' modeled, masking behavior and copy it anyway. Effectively, they learn how to mask their own behavior.

Masking for a student might be that the student is a very poor reader and in danger of failing and covers it up with acting-out behaviors, such as refusing to work, talking to others, or disturbing the class. She really does not want to act out or disappoint the teacher, but she feels her mask is necessary to protect her self-esteem and her need for the approval and regard of her peers. It is clear that to be more effective, teachers must reveal their masks to themselves. This first step of unmasking is to observe their interaction in the classroom and with other teachers. When they recognize that some dissonance is apparent, journaling about it could help unmask those feelings.

This step is critical for unmasking behaviors that students may try to mirror, such as self-doubt and lack of confidence. Introspective, quiet time alone could be useful for helping teachers unmask their true feelings. Once the masked feelings are uncovered, teachers should overhaul their belief systems and replace false truths with a more realistic, authentic set of truths that will not be easily masked. Finally, teachers can turn to their spiritual faith and seek ways to reveal their problems and facilitate healing. The foundation for any truth-seeking is to first acknowledge that some things are not fine; for example, teachers who constantly make excuses for themselves may be covering up facts that they prefer to deny.

Hanson (2013), a neuroscientist, proposes that negative experiences stay with us more so than positive experiences. This is a legacy of the brain of early humans that was necessary for survival. If negatives were strong memories, it would reduce the likelihood that humans would experience a repeat of the negatives. This survival tactic is still present in today's thinking. Teachers who entertain self-doubt obviously hold on to the negatives and pay less attention to positive experiences. Neurologically, self-doubting teachers can create positive neural pathways just like they created negative pathways. Positive thinking can replace negative thinking and minimize masking behavior while promoting a can-do attitude.

Teachers can develop a can-do attitude by looking on the bright side of perceived dark situations. Self-talk, such as daily affirmations of personal skills and attributes, also can be effective. Teachers can enhance their can-do attitude by embracing criticism as helpful advice. Once teachers have removed their masks of self-doubt and replaced them with masks of can-do, there are numerous ways teachers can help students put on their can-do masks:

- Encourage students to use divergent thinking to solve problems.
- Encourage students to use inquiry and investigation as tools of learning.
- Employ discovery learning techniques when appropriate.
- Encourage students to respectfully challenge ideas and the status quo and not take it personally when they do.
- Encourage students to take a stance on issues that are developmentally appropriate.
- Encourage students to research and find evidence to support their beliefs, theories, and interpretations.
- Encourage children to value their own ideas and thoughts, listen to them, and respond appropriately.
- Encourage students to represent their point of view without fear of criticism.
- Encourage students to articulate their preferences when appropriate.
- Encourage students to speak and contribute at length when possible.

GIVE YOUR EMOTIONAL IQ A BLASTOFF

The term *emotional intelligence* intuitively suggests intelligence that is involved with emotion. This term was first introduced in an ability model by Yale psychologists Salovey and Mayer (1990), who explained that intelligence is the capacity to reason validly about something. Much like the logical-mathematical, verbal, and other intelligences proposed by Gardner (1983), they contend that emotional intelligence involves reasoning with the emotions.

Emotional intelligence is a measure of our ability to interact and relate to others appropriately and to discriminate between emotions and label them properly. The process involves becoming aware of our feelings and what they truly mean and accurately perceiving the feelings of others. Emotional intelligence is important for regulating emotional thoughts and subsequent behaviors. For example, a teacher may misread a student's comment as a sarcastic remark and have an inappropriate emotional reaction to the comment, such as angry yelling.

Having emotional intelligence allows a person to interpret emotional signals given off by others and respond in a harmonious, balanced fashion. It also will cue us on how our emotions and behaviors will affect those around us and how others' behaviors are affecting us. The benefits of emotional intelligence are many. Improved mental health is certainly one. A good sense of emotional intelligence decreases the likelihood of having a highly stress-laden reaction to minor incidences, which could have a negative effect on mental and physical health.

Having a healthy balance of emotional intelligence may be influenced by the area of the brain that is used to reason out a response to a situation. Barbey, Colom, and Grafman (2012) found that regions in the frontal cortex and parietal cortex were important to both general and emotional intelligence. The emotional area of the brain affects our decision making and our ability to manage our emotions and understand human behavior, body language, and social cues. Fortunately, having emotional intelligence can make our decisions more rational and help us effectively manage our emotions in a positive manner and more accurately identify the feelings of ourselves and others.

Whether emotional intelligence is genetic or environmental is still a source of debate. Skottke (2005) says that changes in human intelligence may be explained by genetics; however, many environmental factors influence intelligence. Logically, emotional intelligence as a type of intelligence is also influenced by both genes and environment. Much can be learned about emotional intelligence.

We can learn to be less reactive or impulsive and be more willing to think matters through when we encounter conflict or a problem. We can distinguish between conflicting feelings and decode the true source of the current feeling with introspection and practice. We can determine the most appropriate response from many possible responses, basing our decisions on the consequences of past learning experiences. We can learn to diffuse or change the emotions of others. For example, conferencing with an angry parent can be a difficult task, but choosing to empathize with the parent, assuming that the parent has had a long, stressful day, could sufficiently diffuse the parent's anger and result in a positive, productive conference. Goleman (1995) argues that emotional intelligence may be more important than IQ. Exercise 9.3 offers some strategies for enhancing emotional intelligence.

ADVANCING YOUR LEADERSHIP ABILITIES: LEAD SOMETHING

Teachers are presented with opportunities to lead in a variety of venues, such as leading collegial activities, parent activities, or administrative or community projects. Effective leadership minimizes conflict with students, parents, administration, and the community. The beneficial outcomes may be more student engagement, fewer dropouts, more parent involvement, and improved relationships with administration.

A great teacher-leader may encourage more parent and community involvement. Teacher-leaders are not born; they evolve as the teacher practices the principles of leadership at every opportunity. The old model of teaching was very authoritarian; teachers told students what to do and used various modes of punishment to make sure they did it. As a result, many students resented and resisted harsh discipline models. Some students simply dropped out because they did not like school and/or their ineffective teachers.

Hunter (2012) proposes that leadership skills can be learned and applied by most people if they're willing to grow and change. For teachers to grow and become effective leaders, they must first become aware of good leadership skills, embrace them, and practice them often to improve. Understanding the qualities, traits, and practices of a good leader are critical to successful leadership. A definition for leadership might be a caring, competent, charismatic person with integrity who can move people to action to achieve a goal.

Characteristics of a good teacher-leader are the selected operational components of the definition of leadership. The teacher-leader would be caring in that she cares about students and quality outcomes. The charismatic teacher fosters good relationships with parents, students, colleagues, and the community. Confidence, including high expectations of success and high self-efficacy, also are characteristics of good teacher-leaders. The inspiring teacher-leader can get others excited about an idea or project and more willing to work to get the job done. This type of teacher-leader helps others feel ownership and satisfaction, making others aspire to be like her.

This great teacher-leader is goal oriented, meaning that she is well organized and can conceptualize a means to an end and follow through until the end. Teacher-leaders are competent; they are able to handle tasks effectively and efficiently. They are highly intelligent and flexible, and they strive for excellence using their strong problem-solving capabilities.

Having a great leadership style will help teachers move more students to action, encourage more parents to get involved, and garner more support from administration. As the teacher-leader progresses at perfecting her leadership skills, she should take advantage of the myriad opportunities to lead offered in the school setting. Teacher-leaders can take the lead in planning and setting up art or science fairs, create student programs to showcase students' talents for parents, and lead the school cleanup campaign and invite the community. There are many opportunities to lead, and these are just a few examples.

REFERENCES

Barbey, A. K., Colom, R., & Grafman, J. (2012). Distributed neural system for emotional intelligence revealed by lesion mapping. *Social Cognitive and Affective Neuroscience Advance Access*. http://www.decisionneurosciencelab.org/pdfs/Soc%20Cogn%20Affect%20Neurosci-2012-Barbey-scan_nss124.pdf

deCharms, R. (1977). Pawn or origin? Enhancing motivation in disaffected youth. *Educational Leadership*, *34*(6), 444–448.

Gardner, H. (1983). *Frames of mind: the theory of multiple intelligences*. New York: Basic Books.

Goleman, D. (1995). *Emotional intelligence*. New York: Bantam.

Hanson, R. (2013). *Hardwiring happiness: The new brain science of contentment, calm, and confidence*. NewYork: Crown.

Hunter, J. C. (2012). *The servant: A simple story about the true essence of leadership*. New York: Random House.

Maslow, A. H. (1968). *Toward a psychology of being*. New York: Wiley.

Rotter, J. B. (1975). Some problems and misconceptions related to the construct of internal versus external control of reinforcement. *Journal of Consulting and Clinical Psychology*, *43*(1), 56–67.

Salovey, P., & Mayer, J. D. (1990). *Emotional intelligence*. Amityville, NY: Baywood.

Skottke, K. R. (2005). The evolution of human intelligence: Increasing importance of domain-specific intelligence in the modern environment. *Great Ideas in Personality*. http://www.personalityresearch.org/papers/skottke.html

Smith, V. (2004). Empowering teachers: Empowering children? How can researchers initiate and research empowerment? *Journal of Research in Reading*, *27*(4), 413–424.

Wilson, S. M. (1993). The Self-Empowerment Index: A measure of internally and externally expressed teacher autonomy. *Educational and Psychological Measurement*, *53*, 727–737.

Exercise 9.1: Releasing the Sweet Fruits of Power in You and Your Students

Instructions: Teachers can help students break through their sharp spiky, exterior of self-doubt to embrace their inner powers of tenacity, nonconformity, ingenuity, multiple talents, and resourcefulness; much like peeling through difficult fruit to taste the sweet interior. Write examples of ways you can help students discover their inner powers.

Durian		How can you empower your students to be tenacious and persevere beyond unpleasantness?
Jack Fruit		How can you empower your students to go beyond ugly situations to embrace the wonderful fruit of nonconformity?
Snake Fruit		How can you empower your students to develop ingenious strategies for getting around sharp, painful situations?
Mangosteen		How can you empower your students to release their multiple talents within?
Rambutan		How can you empower students to tap into their inner resourcefulness?

 **Exercise 9.2: Unmasking Your Doubts and Your Students' Doubts with a Can-Do Attitude**

Instructions: For the mask exercise, list the lies that you may be masking. For example, telling other teachers that you don't care what your students think of you when the truth being masked by that lie is that you are afraid that your students don't respect or care for you. Perform the following tasks in column #1 that focuses on eradicating your self-doubt, exploring truths behind the masked lies and finally, eradicating masked lies by taking action that promotes a can-do attitude. State explicitly what action you can take in task #2. Next, in column 2 list ways you can encourage children to perform the same exercise.

Unmasking Your Doubts	Unmasking Your Students' Doubts
Is Your Protective Mask Telling Lies? Lie #1 _____ Lie #2 _____ Lie #3 _____	Are Your Students' Masks Telling Lies? Lie #1 _____ Lie #2 _____ Lie #3 _____
Focus on You	**Focus on Your Students**
1. Spend 4–5 minutes and think about the truths behind the masked lies. Task #1 Record your observations _____ Task #2 What action will you take? _____	1. Encourage students to think about their masked lies and the truths behind them. Task #1 Have them record their observations _____ Task #2 Help them determine what action to take _____
2. Examine your views about your areas of self-doubt. Task #1 List pros and cons of each doubt _____ Task #2 What action will you take? _____	2. Help students to examine their views about their areas of doubt. Task #1 Have them list pros and cons of each doubt. _____ Task #2 Help them determine what action to take? _____

Exercise 9.2: Unmasking Your Doubts (continued)

3. Try to bring awareness to hidden feelings about your doubts. Task #1 Brainstorm possibilities _____ Task #2 What action will you take?_____	3. Try to help students bring awareness to hidden feelings about their doubts. Task #1 Help them to brainstorm possibilities _____ Task #2 Help them determine what action to take_____
4. Take the focus off of your self-doubts and think about your relationships with others. Task #1 List ways your doubts are self-centered _____ Task #2 What action will you take?_____	4. Help students take the focus off of their self-doubts and think about their relationships with others. Task #1 Help them to list ways their doubts are self-centered _____ Task #2 Help them determine what action to take _____
5. Reflect on the importance of others in your self-doubts. Task #1 Record your observations _____ Task #2 What action will you take?_____	5. Help students to reflect on the importance of others in their self- doubts. Task #1 Help them to record their observations _____ Task #2 Help them determine what action to take_____
6. Reflect on people in your social circle that make you feel you "can do" things well. Task #1 Rank 10 of those people and pledge to contact at least the top five _____ _____ Task #2 What action will you take?_____	6. Help students to reflect on people in their social circle that make them feel they "can do" things well. Task #1 Rank 10 of those people and pledge to contact at least the top five _____ _____ Task #2 Help them determine what action to take _____
7. Change your environment to encourage a can-do attitude. Task #1 Inventory your surroundings for areas needing change _____ _____ Task #2 What action will you take?_____	7. Help students to change their environment to encourage a can-do attitude. Task #1 Help them to inventory their surroundings _____ _____ Task #2 Help them determine what action to take _____

Exercise 9.3: Blastoff Your Emotional Intelligence Skills In 5 Days

Instructions: This exercise is designed to enhance your emotional intelligence skills in five days. For day one, choose a relevant tip from the list of "*Tips for Enhancing Your Emotional Intelligence*" that follows. When you have successfully employed that tip put the number of the tip in the day one box. Repeat the process for day 2, increasing the number of tips to two and recording the corresponding number of the 2 employed tips in the day 2 boxes. Keep repeating the process and increasing the tips until day 5. By day five, you will have increased your emotional intelligence awarenesses and skills significantly.

Day 5

Day 4

Day 3

Day 2

Day 1

				Tip # _____
			Tip # _____	Tip # _____
		Tip # _____	Tip # _____	Tip # _____
	Tip # _____	Tip # _____	Tip # _____	Tip # _____
Tip # _____	Tip # _____	Tip # _____	Tip # _____	Tip # _____

Exercise 9.3: Blastoff Your Emotional Intelligence (continued)

Tips For Enhancing Your Emotional Intelligence

Tip #1. Clarify a conflict situation before acting on it.
Tip #2. Use self-talk to ask yourself what you are feeling.
Tip #3. Give students a clean slate each day; avoid dwelling on past behavior.
Tip #4. Take 5 minutes to think of potential sources of stress in the classroom.
Tip #5. Make an overture of peace with a coworker who disagreed with your ideas.
Tip #6. Smile and tell yourself you feel happy at least three times a day and note your feelings.
Tip #7. Help diffuse student anger by listening calmly without interruption before speaking.
Tip #8. When a student or coworker is upset, try to read between the lines and hear what they are not saying.
Tip #9. Test your assessment of what classroom activities students enjoy by comparing your rating to their anonymous ratings. If there are surprises, make changes.
Tip #10. Tell yourself why your heart is racing or why your stomach is in knots; make a note to alleviate the source of stress.
Tip #11. Ask for a reality check from a trusted coworker if you suspect you are overreacting to a situation.
Tip #12. Distract negativity with positive action.
Tip #13. Yield your rights in an argument or contentious situation that is not important to your well-being.
Tip #14. Avoid raising your voice if your classroom seems to be out of control; try silence until you get silence.
Tip #15. Try some free-association writing on the problems you perceive in your classroom to help you develop an action plan.
Tip #16. Assertively say no to unacceptable student behavior and do not entertain guilt or doubt feelings about doing so.
Tip #17. When you feel upset about a student's behavior, smile and smile some more to trick your brain into believing you're feeling fine; note your feelings.
Tip #18. Try to read students' looks in a positive light. What may appear to be disinterest or disrespect may in fact be a headache.
Tip #19. Avoid personalizing and internalizing student behaviors. If a student fails to turn in homework she may not be blowing off your assignment, there may have been a family emergency. Inquire.
Tip #20. If a student is doing something that is irritating you, breathe for 30 seconds before choosing an appropriate course of action.
Tip #21. Resist the urge to impulsively send emotional communications to parents, coworkers or administration. Write it, think about it, rewrite a more positive version before sending it.

 **Exercise 9.4: How Do Your Leadership Skills Stack Up?**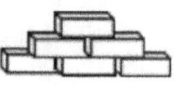

Instructions: Darken in the number of bricks that reflect your perception of your leadership skills on a scale from 1-6 with 1 being very low and 6 being very high.

Leadership Characteristics	1	2	3	4	5	6
Caring						
Charisma						
Confidence						
Goal-oriented						
Competent						
Inspiring						
Organized						
Focused						
Trustworthy						
Responsible						
Respectful						
Team Player						
Problem Solver						
Motivator						
Communication Skills						
Total						

90-80 Excellent Leader 4 Stacks

79-60 Strong Leader 3 Stacks

59-40 Average Leader 2 Stacks

39-0 Poor Leader 1 Stack

10

Changing Inside and Out
Necessary Steps for Being the Best

Sorry Babe, I would change for you if I could.

The world can only change from within.

—Eckhart Tolle

ACCEPTING THE INEVITABILITY OF CHANGE

Recently in the news, a volcano in Hawaii erupted and did a slow, hot, snaky dance down the hillside, inching ever closer to homes and changing everything in its path to lava rock. Reporters said that home owners calmly packed up to move, knowing they were not likely to see their homes again. They knew and accepted what few are willing to accept: that change is inevitable. Most of them said that living near a volcano meant that it could erupt at any time and that their lives would change in an instant. They were able to accept the inevitability of change because they had accepted that they would simply adapt if the volcano ever erupted in their lifetime.

Educators must acknowledge that they have experienced a powerful, digital eruption and that education as they have known it for previous decades is in the path of imminent change. The dawning of the information age and the Internet has exploded onto the world, spewing out social media, online banking, e-books, smart phones, and online education, to name a few. The encroaching hot-tech mix is smoldering and reshaping the landscape of education, making it almost unrecognizable compared to the way it looked decades ago.

Social media have changed the way we communicate. The lament of teachers about students for decades was that "they won't stop talking." In the 21st century, most students don't really talk to each other; they prefer to text (this is especially true of older students). They would prefer to gaze at a smartphone wearing headphones and enjoying video clips, humorous postings, and pictures of people rather than interact with live people. Today, many students have lost the art of conversation; handwriting, hard-copy books, chalkboards, and writing pens are rapidly becoming relics of a bygone era.

Lunch money is no longer collected; it is paid for by credit card online or through phones that use fingerprint recognition to pay through an intermediary. Hard-copy books give way to e-books, allowing students to read from their phones anywhere and at any time. Video clips are an integral part of student readings that are in electronic formats. Students no longer need the classroom library. Hundreds of books are stored on their tablets and other e-readers.

Musical instruments are no longer needed; beats, vocals, and music are easily assembled on computer to create instant, easy music. Digital music is easily accessible and in many cases free. Understandably, CDs, vinyl records, and video- and audiotapes are practically obsolete. The classroom that features chalkboards or whiteboards is outdated. Smart boards connected to a computer or computer network, when they are affordable, are the preferred options. Parent contact is rarely in person, as teachers prefer e-mail. A mini parent conference may be set up using Facetime on the phone or Skype on the computer.

Students are very technology oriented; they know how to surf the Internet to find new information. Some students are looking up the information as fast as teachers are presenting the topic to the class. If the teacher makes an error, she is immediately challenged with the findings from the Internet. Online learning is diminishing the need for many classrooms because online, asynchronous instruction allows students to view videos of teachers teaching, animated demonstrations, and video clips of educational content complete with online assessment. The much-feared red pen, used for grading papers in the past with red checkmarks, are passé, being replaced by electronic vocal feedback and electronic grading.

Rather than play or interact with other students, some students prefer to take pictures of themselves in various settings and send them to other students and wait with bated breath to see if anyone in cyberspace "likes" their pictures. Student cliques are now online as followers; apparently, student self-worth is often assessed by the number of followers or likes they receive. A Chinese proverb says that "when the winds of change blow, some build walls while others build windmills."

Teachers must build windmills to accommodate the impending changes in education. They must do something different for change to occur, and they can't wait for someone else to do it. They must get ahead of the digital lava flow that threatens to engulf them. Change is not easy; people tend to resist change and find it hard to let go of the known. Letting go is a necessary fight with the self to move forward out of the lava path. The new change must not be trying to find innovative ways to continue to do the same things that were done in the traditional education model of the past 100 years.

On the contrary, the new change must be visionary, reinventing, reshaping, and innovative. To adapt, teachers must learn to embrace change and to change themselves as they brainstorm ways to accommodate the Internet effect on education. Exercise 10.1 provides a guide for making changes. Be innovative!

TRANSFORMING YOURSELF AND EMBRACING CHANGE

John Dewey was an important change agent for American education who brought together two opposing perspectives of education that were prevalent in the early 19th century. The view of formal, traditional education was viewed by some as the antithesis of progressive learning from discovery and experience. Dewey proposed that real experience could be synthesized with academic learning, making formal education better (Dewey & Cohen, 1988). Dewey advocated change in various aspects of traditional education. He was concerned that schools did not sufficiently interact with the real world.

The role of the teacher was enforcer, the quiet classroom or stillness and silence reigned. The fact that the material was presented without context, purpose, and grounding in real-life experience was of particular concern. Dewey thought that the solution to improving American education would be found in continuous adaptation and incorporation of experiential learning (Dewey & Cohen, 1988). His historic, profound observations laid the foundation for today's constructivist practices. The prerequisite for change is adaptation.

To facilitate change for the better in education, teachers must embrace change and be willing to transform themselves; much like chameleons make adaptations to situations by changing their color, teachers must be willing to transform themselves to adapt to situations. A chameleon provides a good model for teacher change in a variety of ways. Contrary to popular belief, for chameleons color change is a communication display rather than a camouflage. Color changes are adaptations or responses to situations, attitudes, and moods. Humans are blessed with color vision, making it possible to view colors associated with human moods and attitudes.

A blush is a giveaway communication that the person may be feeling shame or embarrassment. Recognizing that emotions can be communicated by color gives teachers a unique opportunity to examine the colors they are communicating to students and change them if they're not positive.

Certain colors have been associated with communicating feelings in humans, such as a red face for anger or white for fear or panic; people say that a person is green with envy or is having a blue or dark mood. Yellow may signal illness, whereas pink is often associated with health. Students can see frustration on a teacher's red, angry face. They can detect a white pallor of fear when a teacher is nervous or fearful. Reciprocal "color" reading of communications between teachers and students can help avoid conflict and power struggles and help determine opportune times for positive interactions. Students may be more cooperative and respectful if they detect that the teacher is in a blue mood or be repelled into silence if they detect a black or red mood.

Some colors have been associated with traits as well, such as purple for power, yellow for happiness, and red for love. Develop your color profile using the table 10.1 and exercise 10.2. First, add colors of your choosing for the 26 positive traits in table 10.1. Feel free to use other positive traits if they are more relevant for you and associate them with any color. Next, in exercise 10.2, use the colors and traits from the table that describe you as a guide to developing your own chameleon color profile that will facilitate a colorful change in you.

BREAKING THE WALTZ OF OLD HABITS AND LEARNING TO SALSA WITH NEW ONES

A definition of learning is acquiring information from experiences that endure over time and that are not due to maturation (Schunk, 2012). Through the years, the tools of learning have been simple: a book, paper, pencil, chalk, a blackboard, reference books, maps, and a teacher to facilitate the use of these tools for learning. A typical traditional learning scenario might be to have students in a classroom

Table 10.1. Positive Traits and Associated Colors

Instructions: Associate the following traits with a color that you think is most representative of that trait. You may use a color more than once if you choose. Use this completed table for exercise 10.2 that follows.			
Trait	*Color Choice*	*Trait*	*Color Choice*
Honest		Wise	
Fair		Humble	
Responsible		Realistic	
Imaginative		Adventurous	
Self-Confident		Spontaneous	
Considerate		Tolerant	
Clever		Inspiring	
Creative		Graceful	
Thoughtful		Bright	
Funny		Loving	
Lighthearted		Optimistic	
Successful		Kind	
Decisive		Cheerful	

- read a passage in a book,
- listen to a teacher explain the passage or organize it in a way to make it more meaningful for the students (Ausubel, 1963),
- give students some questions to answer,
- assess their learning by requiring them to put their answers on a chalkboard, and, finally,
- read their answers to the class.

This manner of teaching endured for about 100 years and tapered off with the advent of computer technology.

In recent years, almost everything has changed; students may read or hear text read to them via vast amounts of information in digital formats, such as e-books and websites, that have been enhanced by authenticating video clips, audio excerpts, 3-D images, and interactive charts and displays. Students no longer have to be in the classroom setting to receive instruction. They can be at home on a computer using distance learning to see a teacher several miles away. They can receive synchronous or asynchronous instruction via course management software. They can chat or discuss online, and their comments or responses will be appropriately threaded to the initiating comment or response.

Presentation is no longer simple recitation; even young children learn to create PowerPoint or Prezi presentations on the computer. Teachers have replaced chalkboards and whiteboards with smart boards that allow teachers to project written notes or help students follow a reading passage on the screen; her students see what she sees. Students no longer pass paper notes to communicate; they can send a text to each other using their smartphones, and the teacher is unaware of it. They can cheat in very sophisticated ways, such as using their cell phones to take a picture of sensitive test questions or information or recording audio using their cell phones.

They don't need to join study groups for some assignments; they snap a picture of their homework and send it out in a text to several people using group messaging. They Google or do an electronic search for information online to get answers from sources such as Wikipedia and online dictionaries. Students can make a video of something happening in the classroom and upload it to YouTube, Facebook, and other forms of social media.

Some teachers may have doubts about their competencies in a digital learning world using digital tools. The pendulum of power in learning is shifting to those who possess technological expertise and the ability to employ technical tools for maximum effectiveness and impact. Today's students have an advantage over their teachers, they have no doubts about their ability to use new technologies, and they hunger to explore the mysteries that new technological advances help them unfold. Most teachers proceed with caution and are reluctant to try new technologies for fear of failure and embarrassment.

Their students, however, will continue to advance and use new technologies. Students' continued advancement in using technology will further perpetuate teachers' doubts unless teachers advance themselves and embrace future technologies to become tech savvy and doubt free in this digital learning environment.

NOW THAT YOU BELIEVE: CONSIDER THE POSSIBILITIES

Throughout childhood, children are encouraged to believe in magic, fanciful creatures, superbeings, and mythical people. Children's literature is rife with magic, superpowers, superdeeds, and other such imagery. Children believe in Santa in a flying sleigh, fairy godmothers with superpowers, supermen with X-ray vision and the ability to read minds, and superstrong men who can defeat any foe. *The Wizard of Oz* continues to enamor audiences 80 years after it was first performed. Audiences watch year after year to see again and again how powerful beliefs can be if one follows a yellow brick road full of fantasy and how clicking the heels of one's ruby red slippers makes a topsy-turvy life right again.

Teachers would love to have powers, a crystal ball mind, eyes in the back of their heads, or X-ray vision to see what students are doing at all times and a magic wand to change a pumpkin of a classroom into something beautiful, alive, and highly functional. Teachers would love to have fairy dust to transform difficult students into ideal students. Teachers who believe in magic would whip up lesson potions that would render students excited about learning and fully engaged in constructing new learning and creative ideas.

Unlike childhood, adulthood has a low tolerance for fantasy beliefs. Dreams of Santa, flying reindeer, fairy godmothers, and magic wands become extinct, extinguished from life early on with a huge dose of icy reality. Fortunately, teachers don't have to believe in fantasy and superpowers. They don't have to click their ruby red teacher's slippers. They simply have to learn to believe in themselves.

They don't need a magic potion or a magic wand. They can simply use the three-step believe-in-yourself process to become a power teacher who employs the given strategies and techniques to create a wonderful classroom. Unwavering belief in oneself can be transformative and empowering. Teachers who learn to believe in themselves more become teacher-believers. Witness the three-step believe-in-yourself transformation of Liz in the accompanying feature.

TEACHER INTERVIEW WITH LIZ: USING THE THREE-STEP BELIEVE-IN-YOURSELF PROCESS TO CREATE A TEACHER-BELIEVER

Step 1, the disconnect phase for Liz, whose account of her self-doubts was especially prolific and poignant, revealed that she had self-doubts about EVERYTHING! She was always second-guessing herself, thinking "Was that the correct discipline approach?" or "Was that the best way to teach that lesson, there are so many strategies to choose from?" After ascertaining that the source of much of her doubt was negative messages from her childhood, Liz said, "I was raised by a critical mother and an older sister. Between the two of them, I felt that I never did anything right; they were always right and I was always wrong." Bringing those revelations to consciousness created an awareness of her need for change.

Step 2, the repair and reconnect phase, for Liz revealed a persistent negative thought that she was not good at anything. A deep, belief-repairing, conversational probe revealed that she was artistic and very creative. She also was very good at beading. This revelation was a start for repairing her damaged self-efficacy.

Step 3, the making new connections phase for Liz, was to develop a willingness to change. With encouragement and challenge, Liz agreed to do at least one of the three things that she always wanted to do but felt she could not do. She made a commitment to try dancing as her first task of reinventing herself. She acknowledged that she was indeed a very good dancer. This little bit of success could transfer to her efforts to improve her teaching and her perceptions of her teacher efficacy. She would start to believe in herself more with every successful effort—she would become a teacher-believer.

Teacher-believers, in lieu of having special powers, will develop personal traits that provide them with the ability to handle all aspects of classroom management and teaching less motivated, difficult students. Teacher-believers will think highly of themselves and set lofty, achievable goals for themselves and their students. They will be excellent time managers who will know how to minimize interruptions and increase engaged time in the classroom. Knowledgeable colleagues will be viewed as valued resources and sources of support. Parent involvement will not be an issue; in fact, parents will be seen as assets and welcomed into the classroom. The classrooms of these empowered teachers will be aesthetically pleasing, inviting, well-designed, and well-organized oases of learning.

Teacher-believers will be trendy and open to the latest technological advances in education. They will encourage their students to share what they know and to learn about the latest technology. Being learner-centered and committed to using only the best evidence-based practices available will be their class mission. These teachers will readily harvest interesting, innovative, entertaining teaching strategies from the Internet, educational literature, and professional development seminars to maximize student engagement. Their students will love acquiring an arsenal of skills and coming to class to explore the new ways of learning offered to them.

Teacher-believers will be highly creative, planning interesting lessons that are differentiated, authentic, and meaningful. They will keep discipline problems to a minimum because students will be too busy having fun to be disruptive. They will be able to achieve their desired learning outcomes in spite of the hindrances of high-stakes testing and the demands of school districts to teach to the test. In the process, students will be adequately prepared for their end-of-the-year tests.

Teacher-believers will be empowered with the physical and mental stamina to handle the typical teacher workload because they will pay close attention to their wellness and fitness issues. They realize that being fit models good health and well-being for their students. The emotional intelligence of teacher-believers will be high on the charts. They will approach discipline or classroom management problems with calm assurance. Their high self-efficacy or belief in themselves will power them to successful educational outcomes. They will manage their stressors to avoid frustration and inadvertent damage to children.

Most of all, teacher-believers will be loving and caring. They will not cross the line of caring and friendliness into inappropriate "friendships." The diversity of their students will be viewed as a source of joy for them. Students of all shapes, sizes, colors, needs, and challenges will be embraced by teacher-believers. Their belief in themselves and their students will be unwavering and sustainable throughout the years. They will intuitively know how to motivate the seemingly unmotivated students. Teachers who learn to believe in themselves are transformed as they merge from their cocoon of doubt to spread their wings of confidence and competence and take their places in the classrooms of successful educational outcomes.

PARTING THOUGHTS: A PERSONAL JOURNEY TO BECOMING A TEACHER-BELIEVER

Early in my teaching career, I had a daunting experience. While I was on leave, the fifth-grade team met to divide all of the fifth graders into four classes. Only three of the team teachers participated in the division of students because the fourth class did not have an assigned teacher. When I arrived the day before classes began, I found out that I would be teaching the fourth class. I was greeted by my friend and colleague, who had an anguished, sheepish half grin on her face. "I am so, so sorry"—the words tumbled out before she said hello.

"You have no idea of what we have done to you," she continued. "We did not know you would be teaching the class with no teacher. We put all of the bad kids, the troublemakers and the low achievers, in the class without a teacher; we had no idea that you would be the teacher for that class." I did not feel qualified to handle a class that was filled with so many problem students. I was overcome with doubt as I languished for the next day entertaining a multitude of negative concerns and forebodings.

My first mental gymnastics were to shift from my negative thinking and look for something positive, as in the first step of the three-step believe-in-yourself process. I remembered learning about teacher expectations and how they could easily become a self-fulfilling prophecy causing negative expectations to yield negative results (Rosenthal & Jacobson, 1968). I realized that I had negative expectations of my students and that I had yet to meet them. Step 2 of the three-step process would require that I move beyond my negative expectations.

I wondered what would happen if I could have positive expectations of my students and convince them to see themselves that way; that would be step 3 in the three-step process. I now had an exciting challenge, and I could hardly wait to get started. I became motivated and confident; I wanted to give them a learning environment that would be conducive to a productive school year. I painstakingly created a 3-D bulletin board to welcome students. I greeted my incoming class with a big smile and lots of enthusiasm; they were suspicious and looked at each other with looks of what was going on.

Once they were seated, I said to them, "I am so happy to be your teacher! I heard that I have some of the best students in the school." I'll never forget the incredulous looks on their faces; they looked around and behind themselves as if to see whom I could be referring to, and they could not believe that I was talking to them. These children sorely needed a positive, loving learning experience. I gave them my best, and I believe they gave me their best. My class no longer acted out. They were given a clean slate, interesting instruction, and tender, loving care—the need to act out was gone.

One day, one of the team teachers commented on the way my students behaved when they were returning from recess. "They are so good," she commented. "If I had known they would be this good, I would have kept some of them." I was very proud of their efforts, and I told them so at every opportunity. At the beginning of the school year, all of my students were below grade level on their yearly achievement tests. In an effort to bring them up to grade level, I offered a steak lunch incentive for all students who made grade level and above and dessert for students who showed some improvement. I also gave them plenty of extra tutoring after class.

We had pep rallies to sustain their motivation; I often gave them "eighth-grade work" to boost their self-esteem and confidence. I kept them engaged with some sort of authentic assignment or project as often as possible. At the end of the year, all of my students (except one) were at or above grade level. The student who did not make grade level was so pleased with his improvement and progress toward grade level that he gladly bought his own lunch and accepted my gift of dessert. Everyone was dressed up and feeling great when we embarked on our journey for a well-earned steak lunch at the local steak house.

I was able to overcome my self-doubt and believe in myself more and in the process helping my children believe in themselves. Our classroom, which was once an object of pity, was now a picture of success, maximum engagement, minimum disruption, and higher test scores. Using the three-step believe-in-yourself process, you can do the same. After you have processed the pages of this book, I invite you to embark on a remarkable journey of becoming a teacher-believer and find out what your classroom might look like if you believed in yourself more.

REFERENCES

Ausubel, D. (1963). *The psychology of meaningful verbal learning.* Oxford: Grune & Stratton.

Dewey, J., & Cohen, C. (1988). *The middle works of John Dewey: Essays on politics and society* (Vol. 15). Carbondale: Southern Illinois University Press.

Rosenthal, R., & Jacobson, L. (1968). Pygmalion in the classroom. *The Urban Review*, 3(1), 16–20.

Schunk, D. H. (2012). *Learning theories: An educational perspective.* Upper Saddle River, NJ: Pearson/Merrill Prentice Hall.

Exercise 10.1: Formulary for Change In Education

Instructions: The following stages provide a formula for effecting necessary change related to 21st century classrooms that will be impacted by technology. Think about a current educational practice that will be affected by technology. Fill in the boxes with how you might adapt to the imminent change, step by step. Finally, indicate how you will sustain new changes.

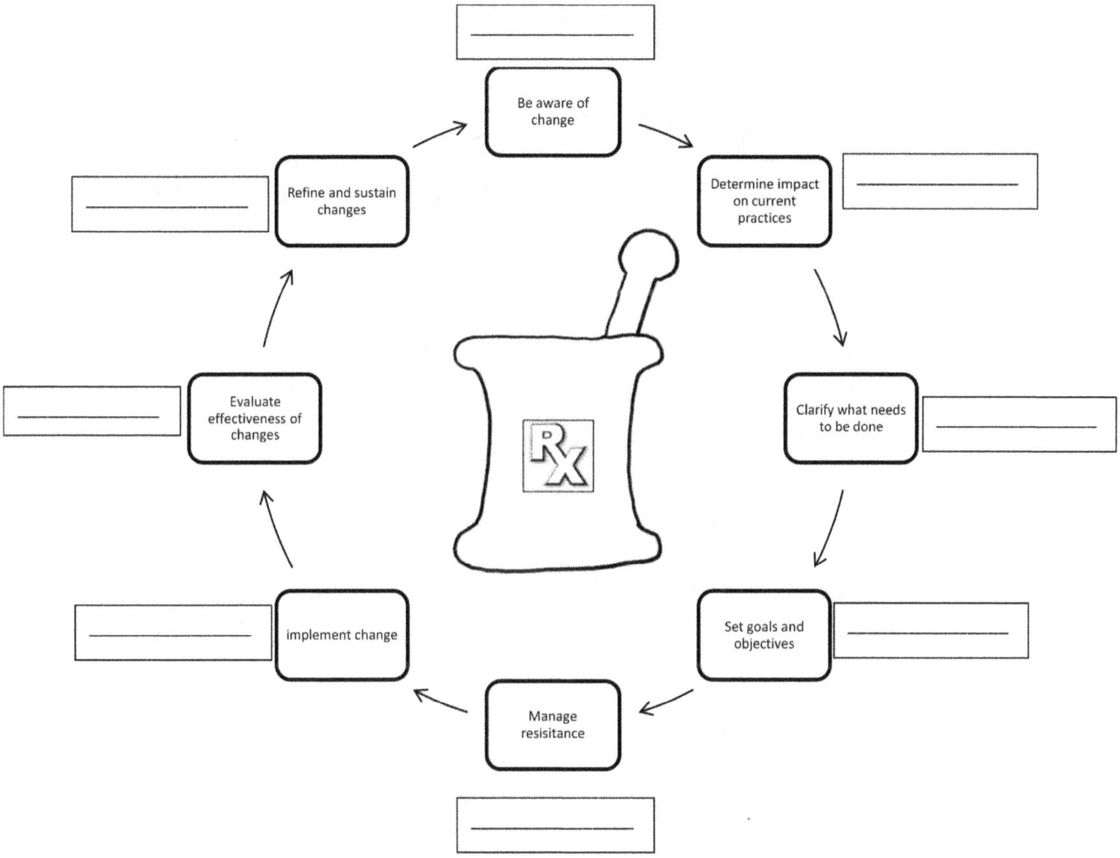

- Be aware of change
- Determine impact on current practices
- Clarify what needs to be done
- Set goals and objectives
- Manage resistance
- implement change
- Evaluate effectiveness of changes
- Refine and sustain changes

Exercise 10.2: Color your Inner Charismatic Chameleon for Change

Instructions: Fill in the blanks with colors and characteristics that are uniquely you that change appropriately or that you would like to see change in various settings. Read the example first; then create your own, putting your name and characteristics in the blanks. Use the previously presented table of positive traits and colors to assist you.

Fred The Charmingly Charismatic Chameleon Is Pure Magic With People.
He displays all of the right colors at the right time with the right people:
Trendy taupe when moving on the fast track with the in-crowd
Gently green and nice in personal interactions,
Popularly purple in the presence of academic royalty,
Ordinary orange and down to earth when it is time to have fun with friends,
Righteous red over injustice toward all people and will not tolerate it,
Blissfully blue when blue skying a new idea with colleagues,
Shrewdly silver and stellar when negotiating with the movers and the shakers.
Stay alert for this Charmingly Charismatic Chameleon called Fred. He is amazing, he may be blending into a crowd anytime, anywhere in the world. Although you may not be able to tell he is there by looking, you will know he is there by his signature laugh, he can't hide that.

_____The Charmingly Charismatic Chameleon Is Pure Magic With _____, displaying all of the right colors at the right time with _____:
_____ when _____
_____ and nice _____
_____ and down to earth when
_____,
_____ over _____,
_____ when _____,
_____ and stellar when
_____.

Stay alert for this Charmingly Charismatic Chameleon called
_____.
___(he/she)_____is amazing, he/she may
be_____
_____
_____
_____
_____
_____
_____
_____
_____
.

Exercise 10.3: Assessment of Teacher Tech Savvy in a Digital Age

Instructions: Test your tech savvy by checking off technological skills and knowledge you already possess and those you need acquire. Give yourself two points for each deal you already possess and one point for each skill that you would like to acquire. If the number of skills you need to acquire is greater than the number of skills you already possess, you should ask for help learning new technologies and add some instructional design and technology classes to your plan for professional development to improve your tech savvy scores.

Points	Yes	No	
	Yes	No	Do you use e-mail on a regular basis?
	Yes	No	Are many of your homework assignments, projects and reading assignments, etc. online for student access?
	Yes	No	Do your students' parents have access to your assignments, grades, and due dates online?
	Yes	No	Do you have a personal website that you created or a website at work that you can update?
			Give yourself a point for each form of social media that you use:
	Yes	No	Facebook
	Yes	No	Twitter
	Yes	No	YouTube
	Yes	No	Instagram
	Yes	No	Other_____
	Yes	No	Other_____
	Yes	No	Do you own a smart phone?
	Yes	No	Have you purchased apps for a smart device such as iPod, iPad, iPhone?
	Yes	No	Do you order products or supplies from companies online?
			Give yourself a point for each one of the following that you own:
	Yes	No	a computer (desktop)
	Yes	No	a laptop computer
	Yes	No	a tablet or iPad
	Yes	No	a smartphone
	Yes	No	a digital camera
			Give yourself a point for each of the following that you use:
	Yes	No	smartphone as a camera or video recorder
	Yes	No	music stored online as a playlist
	Yes	No	readers such as e-books, ibooks, the Nook, or the Kindle
	Yes	No	other
	Yes	No	other
	Yes	No	Do you create PowerPoint presentations?
	Yes	No	Use some form of course management software such as blackboard learn or Moodle?
	Yes	No	Do you use an online grade center for recording grades?
	Yes	No	Do you use an online chat room to to give feedback to students?
	Yes	No	Do you text students and allow them to text you?
	Yes	No	Do you Skype students to give them feedback or instruction?
	Yes	No	Other

Total technology skills you possess_____ vs. Total technology skills you would like to acquire_____

Exercise 10.4. Change Your Future Possibilities with Positive Affirmations

Instructions: A change in thinking usually precedes a change in actions. In a survey, the following statements or concerns and doubts were expressed by preservice and veteran teachers. Choose the statements that reflect your concerns or doubts and change them to positive affirmations by changing them into positive statements of action. The first two concerns are restated as an example. Make a commitment to read over your positive restatements every day for at least 30 days to effect change.

1. **Concerns or Doubts:** Will I lack experience with school policies and rules?
Positive restatement I will take the time to learn all school rules and policies.
2. **Concerns or Doubts:** I might not like or believe in what I teach.
Positive restatement I will be flexible and learn to like and believe in what I teach.
3. **Concerns or Doubts:** Will I be motivated enough to wake up so early in the morning?
Positive restatement _____
4. **Concerns or Doubts:** Will I measure up when compared to other teachers?
Positive restatement _____
5. **Concerns or Doubts:** I fear that I won't be respected because of my young age.
Positive restatement _____
6. **Concerns or Doubts:** Will I find a teaching job and get hired?
Positive restatement _____
7. **Concerns or Doubts:** Will I be able to be fair and unbiased?
Positive restatement _____
8. **Concerns or Doubts:** Will I have the stamina to handle the mental and physical drain of teaching (workload; able to last through the years)?
Positive restatement _____
9. **Concerns or Doubts:** Will I be able to manage and control my classroom or will I get classes that I can't handle; classes that will make me want to quit?
Positive restatement _____
10. **Concerns or Doubts:** Will I be able to negotiate a fair salary?
Positive restatement _____
11. **Concerns or Doubts:** Will I be confident enough to motivate my students?
Positive restatement _____
12. **Concerns or Doubts:** Will I get adequate support from other teachers or administrators?
Positive restatement _____
13. **Concerns or Doubts:** Will I be able to make learning fun (will students enjoy my class; will I make the learning process more enjoyable and interactive)?
Positive restatement _____
14. **Concerns or Doubts:** Will I be able to effectively manage my time?
Positive restatement _____
15. **Concerns or Doubts:** Will I be able to handle the age group that I want to teach (i.e., older children)?
Positive restatement _____

16. **Concerns or Doubts:** Will I be an effective teacher; will I be able to teach them what they need to know and help them to understand the materials?
Positive restatement _____

17. **Concerns or Doubts:** I am concerned that I won't be able to be creative because I have to teach to the test.
Positive restatement _____

18. **Concerns or Doubts:** Will I be able to handle school violence?
Positive restatement _____

19. **Concerns or Doubts:** Will I be well-prepared to teach?
Positive restatement _____

20. **Concerns or Doubts:** Do I have the ability to deal with discipline problems (disruptive classes)?
Positive restatement _____

21. **Concerns or Doubts:** Will I be able to adjust my thinking to understand my students?
Positive restatement _____

22. **Concerns or Doubts:** Will I be able to pass the teacher certification test?
Positive restatement _____

23. **Concerns or Doubts:** Will I be able to handle parents' excessive interference or parents' disengagement?
Positive restatement _____

24. **Concerns or Doubts:** Will I be able to be friendly and not too stern?
Positive restatement _____

25. **Concerns or Doubts:** Will I be able to control my caring so that it is not too much?
Positive restatement _____

26. **Concerns or Doubts:** Will I be able to perform adequately when being observed by my principal?
Positive restatement _____

27. **Concerns or Doubts:** Will I be able to keep feelings of stress and frustration under control?
Positive restatement _____

28. **Concerns or Doubts:** Will I be able to teach a multicultural classroom?
Positive restatement _____

29. **Concerns or Doubts:** I am afraid that I won't know the necessary material or correct grammar, etc.
Positive restatement _____

30. **Concerns or Doubts:** Will I be able to engage my students in ways that will help them to use what I teach them?
Positive restatement _____

31. **Concerns or Doubts:** Will I be able to handle the responsibility of my student's learning?
Positive restatement _____

32. **Concerns or Doubts:** Will I be able to handle inclusion of special needs children and differentiation?
Positive restatement _____

33. **Concerns or Doubts:** Being able to keep students interested (being creative enough).
Positive restatement _____

Index

ability grouping, 52
acceptance, frustration with, 71, 74–75
accurate assessments, with student engagement, 96
adaptation, with change, 119
administration, interrelating with, 16
administrative support, lack of, 19–20
administrators, x
affirmation, of diversity, 87–88
anger: importance of, 70; management of, 69–71; of teachers, 42–43
anger-based conflict, 69
Anger Response Analysis, 80
anxiety. *See* stress and anxiety
approaches, to fears, 6
Are You a Hostage to Self-doubt? 34
arresting, of fears, 10
Assessing Your Star Teacher Persona, 92
Assessment of Teacher Tech Savvy in a Digital Age, 129
assessments: classroom, 53; of teaching, by peers, 56–58
attitude: change in, 40; new, 41; positive, 95; positive influences on, 42–43. *See also* doubt-adverse attitude; humanistic teaching attitude
authentic classroom assessments, 53
avoidance: frustration with, 71, 73–74; of stress and anxiety, 18–20

awareness: frustration with, 71, 72–73; of stress and anxiety, 19

beginning teachers, x, xi, 15
behavioral objectives, 53
behavioral strategy, 70
behavioral traits, of great teachers, 14
behaviorism, 51
believe-in-yourself process, x, xi
benefits, of emotional intelligence, 108
Bennis, Warren, 93
best teaching practices: for effective teacher-pupil interactions, 52; essential, 53; of great teachers, 13–15; for learning, 53–54; for positive discipline, 53; research-tested teaching strategies and, 50; for student development, 51–52; theoretical basis for, 51. *See also* learning theories, best practices mediated by
Blastoff Your Emotional Intelligence Skills in 5 Days, 114–15
Blueprint for Managing Risks Associated with Uncertainty, 68
boosting, of teachers' self-efficacy, 40–43
Boussuet, Jacques BeNigne, 14
bragging, of teachers, 40
brain: mental baggage of, 77; plasticity of, xi; research of, 27

brain-based learning, 53
brainstorm, for teacher evaluation improvement plan, 56

calmness, of teachers, 70–71
change: adaptation relating to, 119; color relating to, 120; with digital music, 118; in education, 118–19; inevitability of, 117–19; old and new habits with, 120–22; with online learning, 118–19; possibilities with, 122–25; with social media, 118; teacher-believer, 125–26; transformation and embracing of, 119–20; as visionary, 119
Change your Future Possibilities with Positive Affirmations, 130–34
characteristics: of interpersonal skills, 86; of leadership abilities, 109
character traits, of great teachers, 14
Check Your "Self-Efficacy," 47
A Child's Conception of the World (Piaget), 4
children: development stages of, 4–5; information processing of, 4; labels for, 4; literal thinking of, 4
classroom: assessments in, 53; environment, cultivation of, 17; greenhouse, 98–100; living and breathing, 98–100; for maximum learning, 98–100
classroom teaching, multidimensionality of, 15
clutter, of mind, 31–32, 35
cognitive strategies, for student engagement, 96
cognitive traits, of great teachers, 14
cognitivism, 51
colleagues, interrelating with, 16
college professors, x
colors, 120, *121*
Color your Inner Charismatic Chameleon for Change, 128

Colton, Charles Caleb, 69
commitment, with student engagement, 96
communication: of flaws, 30–31; good, 87; issues of, 6
comparisons, 5–6, 9
competencies, of teachers, 57
competent student management, 17–18
conceptualization, of anger, 70
constructivism, 51, 97–98
content, of emotional baggage, 78
control, with self-empowerment, 104
Create a Greenhouse Classroom, 102
Create a Tangential Learning Sequence Script, 101
critiques, of teacher evaluations, 56
culturally responsive teaching strategies, 53

debilitating fears, 6–7
definition: of emotional intelligence, 108; of fears, 6; of learning, 120; of self-doubt, ix; of self-efficacy, xiv
denial, 39–40
Developing a Stress-free Model of Teaching, 24
Developing Interpersonal and Intrapersonal Skills, 90–91
development: professional, 20; of students, 51–52; of teacher evaluation improvement plan, 58. *See also* zone of proximal development
developmentally appropriate instruction, 51
development stages, of children, 4–5
Dewey, John, 119
Dick and Jane graded basal readers, 50
differentiated instruction, 53
digital formats, for learning, 121–22
digital music, change with, 118
disconnect phase, ix
discovery learning, 53
diversity, affirmation of, 87–88

documentation, with teacher evaluation improvement plan, 58
doubt: to enlightenment, 85–92; real-world, xi; about teacher evaluations, 54; uprooting of, 11. *See also* self-doubt
doubt, habits of hostage to, 25; assuming negativity, from others, 31; communication, of flaws, 30–31; functional paralysis, 26–27; limited by others, 27–28; listening to incompetent others, 26–27; procrastination, 28–29; seeking comfort of familiarity, 27; self-disparagement, 30–31; self-sabotage, 31; toxic teasing, 29–30
doubt, origins of: comparisons, 5–6, 9; debilitating fears, 6–7; exploration of roots of, 7; negative childhood messages, 3–5; negative childhood whispers, silencing of, 4–5, 8
doubt-adverse attitude: denial, 39–40; procrastination, 43–44; self-efficacy boosted by, 40–43
doubts, empowerment relating to: masking relating to, 105–7; unmasking relating to, 106–7
dynamics, of self-doubt, xvi

education, 118–19
educational environments, for maximum learning, 93–102
educational expenses, out-of-pocket, 20
educators, self-doubt of, xv–xvi
effectiveness: of leadership abilities, 109; of lesson delivery, 17; of teaching, 60
effective teacher-pupil interactions, 52
efficacy: students, xv–xvi, 51; of teachers, xv–xvi, 26, 50. *See also* self-efficacy; self-efficacy, of teachers
embracing, of change, 119–20
emotional baggage, of negative emotions: content of, 78; problems with, 77; professional help for, 78

emotional intelligence: benefits of, 108; definition of, 108; empowerment and, 107–9; as genetic or environmental, 108; importance of, 109
emotions. *See* negative emotions
empowerment, xv; doubts relating to, 105–7; emotional IQ and, 107–9; leadership abilities advanced by, 109–10; potency of, 103–16; self-empowerment, 103–5
encouragement, 87
engagement, of students, 53, 94–98
enlightenment, doubt to, 85–92
enthusiasm, with student engagement, 96
environmental, emotional intelligence as, 108
eradication strategies, for self-doubt, xv
evidence, for teacher evaluation improvement plan, 56, 57
evidence-based teaching, 50
Evidence-based Teaching Evaluations, 65–67
experiences, of self-doubt, x
experiential learning, 119
expert knowledge, of students, 86–87
exploration, of roots of doubt, 7

facilitators, teachers as, 97
familiarity, comfort of, 27
fears: approaches to, 6; arresting of, 10; debilitating, 6–7; definition of, 6; identification of, 10; inequality of, 6–7; of teacher evaluations, 54
feedback, for teacher evaluation improvement plan, 55–56
feelings, of inadequacy, 60
Ford, Henry, 49
Formulary For Change in Education, 127
frustration: with acceptance, 71, 74–75; with avoidance, 71, 73–74; with awareness, 71, 72–73; as negative emotions, 71–75; of teachers, 42–43
functional paralysis, 26–27

genetic, emotional intelligence as, 108
great teacher traits: behavioral, 14; best teaching practices of, 13–15; character, 14; cognitive, 14; personality, 14–15; professional, 15; psychosocial, 15; self-exploration, 13–15
greenhouse classroom, 98–100

habits: with change, 120–22. *See also* doubt, habits of hostage to
hostages: of self-doubt, 25–26, 34. *See also* doubt, habits of hostage to
How do you compare? 9
How Do Your Leadership Skills Stack Up? 116
human flaws, 40
humanistic teaching attitude, 52

idea sharing, 95
identification, of fears, 10
implementation, of teacher evaluation improvement plan, 58
importance: of anger, 70; of emotional intelligence, 109
inadequacy feelings, 60
incivility, 69
individualized instruction, 53
inequality, of fears, 6–7
inevitability, of change, 117–19
influences, on interpersonal skills, 86
information processing, 4, 51
inspiration, 87
instruction: developmentally appropriate, 51; differentiated, 53; individualized, 53
intelligence. *See* emotional intelligence
"intelli-lumens," 88
interactions: with parents, 16; teacher-pupil, 41–42, 52
Internet, 118–19
Internet resources, for teacher evaluation improvement plan, 56–57
interpersonal skills: affirmation, of diversity, 87–88; characteristics of, 86; encouragement, motivation, inspiration, 87; expert knowledge, of students, 86–87; good communication, 87; influences on, 86; love, of teaching, 88; respect, 86; willingness to help students, 87
interrelating, with administration and colleagues, 16

Jacobson, L., 4

Kersey, Cynthia, 103
knowledge. *See* expert knowledge, of students
Korda, Michael, 39

labels, for children, 4
lack: of administrative support, 19–20; of teachers' self-efficacy, 41
leadership abilities: characteristics of, 109; effectiveness of, 109; empowerment and, 109–10
learning: best teaching practices for, 53–54; brain-based, 53; definition of, 120; digital formats for, 121–22; discovery, 53; experiential, 119; online, 118–19; problem-based strategies of, 54; student-centered, 70; tactical experiences of, 95; tangential, 96–98. *See also* maximum learning
learning events, 97–98
learning theories, best practices mediated by, 52–54; behaviorism, 51; cognitivism, 51; constructivism, 51, 97–98; information processing, 51; motivation, 51; social cognitive learning theory, 51
lessons, 17
listening, to incompetent others, 26–27
literal thinking, of children, 4
Lose the Baggage of Negative Thinking and Reclaim your Positive Thinking, 82
love, of teaching, 88
lying, to oneself, 40

Maltz, Maxwell, 25
management: of anger, 69–71; of students, 17–18
masking, of doubts, 105–7
Maslow's hierarchy, 106
maximum learning: educational environments for, 93–102; leaving, breathing classroom for, 98–100; student engagement for, 94–98
mental baggage, of brain, 77
mind, 31–32, 35
mistakes, with teaching, 60–61
mistreatment, of students, 42
motivation, 51, 87
multidimensionality, of classroom teaching, 15
multidirectional sources, of stress and pressure: nonteaching duties, 76; responses to, 76–77; schoolwide, 76; special needs, 75; student personal problems and issues, 75; teacher roles, 76; teaching, 76

negative childhood messages, 3–5
negative childhood whispers, 4–5, 8
negative emotions: anger, 69–71; frustration, 71–75; incivility, 69; losing emotional baggage of, 77–78; stress and pressure, 75–77
negative impacts, of teacher evaluations, 54
negativity, from others, 31
new connect phase, x
nonteaching duties, stress and pressure of, 76

objectives: behavioral, 53; for teacher evaluation improvement plan, 58
observation, of school rules and policies, 16
online learning, change with, 118–19
operative lesson planning, 17
organization, ix–x, 31–32
out-of-pocket educational expenses, stress with, 20

parents, interacting with, 16
peer assessment, of teaching, 56–58
People Events Situations Time Self (PESTS), 11
performance, self-doubt about, xi
personal investment, with student engagement, 96
personality traits, of great teachers, 14–15
personal journey, of teacher-believer, 125–26
PESTS. *See* People Events Situations Time Self
phonics approach, to reading, 50
Piaget, Jean, 4
Piecing Together Best Practices for Better Teaching, 53–54
poll, of veteran teachers, xiii–xiv
poor self-efficacy, 41
positioning, of teachers, 5–6
positive attitude, 95
positive discipline, best teaching practices for, 53
positive influences, on attitude, 42–43
positive outcomes, 43, 50
positive self-affirmation, 8
positive self-efficacy, 27
positive traits and associated colors, *121*
possibilities, with change, 122–25
potency, of empowerment, 103–16
power, with self-empowerment, 104
praise, 52
praise-and-ignore, 70
Preparation Evaluation, 23
preparations: for teacher evaluations, 55, 58. *See also* professional skills and teacher preparation quality
presentations, 58
preservice teachers, x; communication issues of, 6; positioning of, 5–6; survey of, xi–xiii
prevention, of stress and anxiety, 18–19
privacy, 42
problem-based learning strategies, 54

problems: with emotional baggage, 77; of students, 75
procrastination, 28–29, 43–44
Procrastination-Busting Strategies to Get You on a Roll, 48
professional development increase, 20
professional help, for emotional baggage, 78
professional organization, 31–32
professional skills and teacher preparation quality, 15; competent student management, 17–18; cultivating the classroom environment, 17; effective lesson delivery, 17; interacting with parents, 16; interrelating with administration and colleagues, 16; observing school rules and policies, 16; operative lesson planning, 17; proficient in student personnel matters, 18
professional traits, of great teachers, 15
proficiency, in student personnel matters, 18
proliferation, of self-doubt, xiii
psychosocial traits, of great teachers, 15
"Pygmalion in the Classroom" (Rosenthal and Jacobson), 4

questioning, with teaching, 61
quiet, of mind, 31–32

reading, approaches to, 50
real-world doubts, xi
real-world materials and events, for student engagement, 94
Red Heat Rating, 81
Reflections of Truth, 46
regrowing self-efficacy, 41
reinvention, xi
Releasing the Sweet Fruits of Power in You and Your Students, 111
relevance, for appropriate audience, x
remediation, for stress and anxiety, 19
repair and reconnect phase, ix–x

research: of brain, 27; on self-efficacy, xiv
research-based teaching, 50, 51
research-tested teaching strategies, 50
resources and tools, for student engagement, 96
respect, 71, 86
responses, to stress and pressure, 76–77
right things to do, 56–57, 58
risks, of teaching, 59–60
roots, of doubt, exploration of, 7
Rosenthal, R., 4

school rules and policies, observation of, 16
schoolwide sources, of stress and pressure, 76
Schwab, Charles, 85
self-affirmation, positive, 8
self-assurance, x–xi
self-deception, 40
self-disparagement, 30–31
self-doubt: definition of, ix; dynamics of, xvi; of educators, xv–xvi; eradication strategies for, xv; experiences of, x; hostages of, 25–26, 34; about performance, xi; proliferation of, xiii; to self-assurance, x–xi; sources of, ix, xv; universal topic, x
self-efficacy: definition of, xiv; poor, 41; positive, 27; research on, xiv
self-efficacy, of teachers: boosting of, 40–43; lack of, 41; new attitude for, 41; privacy relating to, 42; regrowing, 41; stunted, 40; success and, 40
self-empowerment, 103; control with, 104; power with, 104; tips for, 105
self-esteem promotion, 52
self-evaluation, 56, 57, 61
self-exploration: great teacher traits, 13–15; professional skills and teacher preparation quality, 15–18; stress and anxiety avoidance, 18–20
self-fulfilling prophecies, 30, 52

self-regulated learners, 53
self-sabotage, 31
self-talk, 8
Shakespeare, William, 3
shortcomings and flaws, acknowledgment of, 40
silencing, of negative childhood whispers, 4–5
Silencing Negative Child Whispers, 8
skills. *See* interpersonal skills; professional skills and teacher preparation quality
social cognitive learning theory, 51
social media, change with, 118
sources, of self-doubt, ix, xv
special needs, stress and pressure of, 75
star teacher persona development, 88–89
Steps for Arresting Your Fears, 10
strategies: behavioral, 70; eradication, for self-doubt, xv; learning, problem-based, 54. *See also* teaching strategies
stress, with out-of-pocket educational expenses, 20
stress and anxiety: avoidance of, 18–20; awareness of, 19; increased professional development relating to, 20; with lack of administrative support, 19–20; with out-of-pocket educational expenses, 20; prevention of, 18–19; remediation relating to, 19; with students, 19, 52; of teacher evaluations, 19, 54
stress and pressure, 75–77
stress-free model of teaching. *See* Developing a Stress-free Model of Teaching
student-centered learning, 70
student engagement, 53; accurate assessments with, 96; appropriate resources and tools for, 96; cognitive strategies for, 96; idea sharing with, 95; maximum learning for, 94–98; maximum use of time for, 94; personal investment, enthusiasm, commitment modelled for, 96; positive attitude developed with, 95; real-world materials and events for, 94; tactical learning experiences for, 95; unrestricted inquiry promotion for, 94–95
students: best teaching practices for development of, 51–52; competent management of, 17–18; efficacy, xv–xvi, 51; expert knowledge of, 86–87; help for, 87; mistreatment of, 42; personal problems and issues of, 75; personnel matters of, 18; stress and anxiety with, 19, 52
stunted self-efficacy, 40
success, self-efficacy and, 40
survey, of preservice teachers, xi–xiii
Sweep Away Your Mind Culture, 35

tactical learning experiences, 95
tangential learning, 96–98
teacher-believer: personal journey of, 125–26; three-step believe-in-yourself process for, 123; traits of, 124–25
teacher evaluations: critiques of, 56; doubts about, 54; fear of, 54; negative impacts of, 54; preparations for, 55; stress anxiety with, 19, 54
teacher evaluations, improvement plan for: brainstorm for, 56; development of, 58; documentation with, 58; evidence for, 56, 57; feedback about, 55–56; implementation of, 58; Internet resources for, 56–57; objectives for, 58; peer assessment of teaching, 56–58; preparation for, 58; presentation with, 58; right things to do, 56–57, 58; self-evaluation, 56, 57, 61; teacher competencies for, 57
teacher-pupil interactions, 41–42, 52
teachers: beginning, x, xi, 15; bragging of, 40; calmness of, 70–71; competencies of, 57; efficacy of, xv–xvi, 26, 50; as facilitators, 97; frustration and anger of,

42–43; respect from, 71; shortcomings and flaws of, 40; stress and pressure of roles of, 76; threats to self of, 70–71. *See also* great teacher traits; preservice teachers; professional skills and teacher preparation quality; self-efficacy, of teachers; star teacher persona development; veteran teachers
teaching: classroom, multidimensionality of, 15; effectiveness of, 60; evidence-based, 50; feelings of inadequacy about, 60; humanistic attitude of, 52; love of, 88; managing uncertainties of, 59–61; mistakes with, 60–61; peer assessment of, 56–58; questioning with, 61; research-based, 50, 51; risks of, 59–60; stress and pressure of, 76. *See also* best teaching practices
teaching strategies, 50, 53
test bias, 52
theoretical basis, for best teaching practices, 51
threats, to self, 70–71
three-step believe-in-yourself process, 123
time, maximum use of, 94
tips, for self-empowerment, 105

Tolle, Eckhart, 117
toxic teasing, 29–30
traits: and associated colors, *121*; of teacher-believer, 124–25. *See also* great teacher traits
transformation, with change, 119–20

uncertainties, of teaching, 59–61
understanding, of anger, 70
unmasking, of doubts, 106–7
Unmasking Your Doubts and Your Students' Doubts with a Can-Do, 112–13
unrestricted inquiry promotion, for student engagement, 94–95
Uprooting the Roots of Doubt, 11

veteran teachers, x, xi; poll of, xiii–xiv
visionary, change as, 119
vulnerability disclosure, 40

Wasabi Pea exercise, 22
whole-word approach, to reading, 50
willingness, to help students, 87
The Wizard of Oz, 122

zone of proximal development, 52

About the Author

Carolyn Orange is a professor of educational psychology at the University of Texas, San Antonio, and is the author of *25 Biggest Mistakes Teachers Make and How to Avoid Them* in addition to a number of other books and articles. She is included in *Who's Who in the World*, has received the Yellow Rose of Texas Award in Teaching, and is a member of the San Antonio Women's Hall of Fame.

www.ingramcontent.com/pod-product-compliance
Lightning Source LLC
Chambersburg PA
CBHW080552230426
43663CB00015B/2803